go! CHINESE

听说读打写

Helienke?
Su Lin
Yoong

GO 300

Textbook

(Simplified Character Edition)

罗秋昭
Julie LO

薛意梅
Emily YIH

CENGAGE
Learning™

Andover • Melbourne • Mexico City • Stamford, CT • Toronto • Hong Kong • New Delhi • Seoul • Singapore • Tokyo

Go! Chinese Go300 Textbook
(Simplified Character Edition)
Julie Lo, Emily Yih

Publishing Director, CLT Product Director:
Paul K. H. Tan

Editorial Manager:
Lan Zhao

Associate Development Editor:
Coco Koh

Editor:
Titus Teo

Senior Graphic Designer:
Melvin Chong

Senior Product Manager (Asia):
Joyce Tan

Product Manager (Outside Asia):
Mei Yun Loh

Assistant Publishing Manager:
Pauline Lim

Production Executive:
Cindy Chai

Account Manager (China):
Arthur Sun

Assistant Editor, ELT:
Yuan Ting Soh

For product information and technology assistance, contact us at
Cengage Learning Asia Customer Support, 65-6410-1200

For permission to use material from this text or product,
submit all requests online at **www.cengageasia.com/permissions**
Further permissions questions can be emailed to
asia.permissionrequest@cengage.com

ISBN-13: 978-981-4246-46-0
ISBN-10: 981-4246-46-8

Cengage Learning Asia Pte Ltd
5 Shenton Way #01-01
UIC Building
Singapore 068808

Cengage Learning is a leading provider of customized learning solutions with office locations around the globe, including Andover, Melbourne, Mexico City, Stamford (CT), Toronto, Hong Kong, New Delhi, Seoul, Singapore, and Tokyo. Locate your local office at **www.cengage.com/global**

Cengage Learning products are represented in Canada by Nelson Education, Ltd.

For product information, visit **www.cengagesasia.com**

Printed in Singapore
2 3 4 5 14 13 12 11

Acknowledgements

Go! Chinese is designed to be used together with *IQChinese Go* courseware, a series of multimedia CD-ROM developed by **IQChinese**. We sincerely thank **Wu, Meng-Tien** (Instruction Manager, IQChinese) and **Lanni Wang** (Instruction Specialist, IQChinese) for their tremendous editorial support and advice throughout the development of this program.

We also like to thank the following individuals who offered many helpful insights, ideas, and suggestions for improvement during the product development stage of *Go! Chinese*.

- **Jessie Lin Brown**, Singapore American School, Singapore
- **Henny Chen**, Moreau Catholic High School, USA
- **Yeafen Chen**, University of Wisconsin-Milwaukee, USA
- **Christina Hsu**, Superior Education, USA
- **Yi Liang Jiang**, Beijing Language and Culture University, China
- **Yan Jin**, Singapore American School, Singapore
- **Kerman Kwan**, Irvine Chinese School, USA
- **Chi-Chien Lu**, IBPS Chinese School, USA
- **Andrew Scrimgeour**, University of South Australia, Australia
- **James L. Tan**, Grace Christian High School, the Philippines
- **Man Tao**, Koning Williem I College, the Netherlands
- **Chiungwen Tsai**, Westside Chinese School, USA
- **Tina Wu**, Westside High School, USA
- **YaWen (Alison) Yang**, Concordian International School, Thailand

Preface

Go! Chinese, together with **IQChinese Go** multimedia CD-ROM, is a fully-integrated Chinese language program that offers an easy, enjoyable, and effective learning experience for learners of Chinese as a foreign language.

The themes and lesson plans of the program are designed with reference to the American National Standards for Foreign Language Learning developed by ACTFL[1], and the Curriculum Guides for Modern Languages developed by the Toronto District Board of Education. The program aims to help beginners develop their communicative competence in the four language skills of listening, speaking, reading, and writing while gaining an appreciation of the Chinese culture, exercising their ability to compare and contrast different cultures, making connections with other discipline areas, and extending their learning experiences to their home and communities.

The program employs innovative teaching methodologies and computer applications to enhance language learning, as well as keep students motivated in and outside of the classroom. The CD-ROM companion gives students access to audio, visual, and textual information about the language all at once. Chinese typing is systematically integrated into the program to facilitate the acquisition and retention of new vocabulary and to equip students with a skill that is becoming increasingly important in the Internet era wherein more and more professional and personal correspondence are done electronically.

Course Design

The program is divided into two series: Beginner and Intermediate. The Beginner Series, which comprises four levels (Go100-400), provides a solid foundation for continued study of the Intermediate Series (Go500-800). Each level includes a student text, a workbook, and a CD-ROM companion.

Beginner Series: Go100 – Go400

Designed for zero beginners, each level of the Beginner Series is made up of 10 colorfully illustrated lessons. Each lesson covers new vocabulary and simple sentence structures with particular emphasis on listening and speaking skills. In keeping with the communicative approach, a good mix of activities such as role play, interviews, games, pair work, and language exchanges are incorporated to allow students to learn to communicate through interaction in the target language. The CD-ROM uses rhythmic chants, word games, quizzes, and Chinese typing exercises to improve students' pronunciation, mastery of *pinyin*, and their ability to recognize and read words and sentences taught in each lesson.

The Beginner Series can be completed in roughly 240 hours (160 hours on Textbook and 80 hours on CD-ROM). Upon completion of the Beginner Series, the student will have acquired approximately 500 Chinese characters and 1000 common phrases.

Intermediate Series: Go500 – Go800

The Intermediate Series continues with the use of the communicative approach, but places a greater emphasis on Culture, Community, and Comparison. Through stories revolving around Chinese-American families, students learn vocabulary necessary for expressing themselves in a variety of contexts, describing their world, and discussing cultural differences.

The Intermediate Series can be completed in roughly 320 hours (240 hours on Textbook and 80 hours on CD-ROM). Upon completion of both the Beginner and Intermediate Series, the student will have acquired approximately 1000 Chinese characters and 2400 common phrases.

---

[1] American Council on the Teaching of Foreign Languages (http://www.actfl.org)

Vocabulary and Sentence Structures

The program places emphasis on helping students use the target language in contexts relevant to their everyday lives. Therefore, the chosen vocabulary and sentence structures are based on familiar topics such as family, school activities, hobbies, weather, shopping, food, pets, modes of transport, etc. The same topics are revisited throughout the series to reinforce learning, as well as to expand on the vocabulary and sentence structures acquired before.

Listening and Speaking

Communicative activities encourage and require a learner to speak with and listen to other learners. Well-designed and well-executed communicative activities can help turn the language classroom into an active and enjoyable place where learners are motivated to learn and can learn what they need. The program integrates a variety of communicative activities such as role play, interviews, games, pair work, and language exchanges to give students the opportunity to put what they have learned into practice.

Word Recognition and Reading

Each lesson introduces about 12 new Chinese characters. Using the spiral approach, each new character is first introduced and then recycled in classroom activities and subsequent lessons to enhance retention of new vocabulary over time. *Pinyin* (phonetic notation) is added above newly introduced characters so that students can learn to pronounce them. To make sure students do not become over-reliant on *pinyin* to read Chinese, recycled vocabulary is stripped of *pinyin* so that students can learn to recognize and read the actual written characters in due course. For the same reason, the CD-ROM companion does not display the *pinyin* of words automatically.

Type-to-Learn Methodology

The unique characteristic of this series is the use of Chinese typing as an instructional strategy to improve listening, pronunciation, and word recognition. Activities in the CD-ROM require students to type characters or sentences as they are read aloud or displayed on the computer screen. Students will be alerted if they make a mistake and will be given the chance to correct them. If they do not get it right on the third try, the software provides immediate feedback on how to correct the error. This interactive trial-and-error process allows students to develop self-confidence and learn the language by doing.

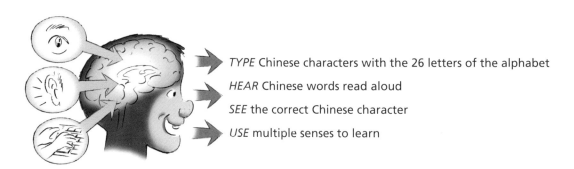

TYPE Chinese characters with the 26 letters of the alphabet

HEAR Chinese words read aloud

SEE the correct Chinese character

USE multiple senses to learn

Chinese Characters and Character Writing

The program does not require the student to be able to hand-write all the core vocabulary; the teacher may however assign more character writing practice according to his or her classroom emphasis and needs. What the program aims to do is to give students a good grasp of Chinese radicals and stroke order rules, as well as to help students understand and appreciate the characteristics and formation of Chinese characters. The program includes writing practice on frequently used characters. Understanding the semantic function radicals have in the characters they form and having the ability to see compound characters by their simpler constituents enable students to memorize new characters in a logical way.

Using the CD-ROM as an Instructional Aid

The following diagram shows how a teacher might use the CD-ROM as an instructional aid to improve traditional classroom instruction.

Textbook   *Multimedia CD-ROM*

Segment 1
(1st class hour)

WARM-UP
Arouse students' interest and set the tone for the whole lesson

Get Started—Additional topic-related words to expand students' vocabulary for daily conversation

Segment 2
(2nd class hour)

Let's CHANT
Rhyming text to be read aloud

Segment 3
(3rd class hour)

Let's Learn GRAMMAR
Grammar

Segment 4
(4th class hour)

Let's TALK
Scripted dialogue practice that may be extended or modified

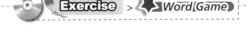

Let's Learn CHARACTER   Let's Learn RADICAL   Let's Learn PUNCTUATION
Learn about Chinese characters, radicals, and punctuation

Segment 5
(5th class hour)

Let's READ
Reading and comprehension

Let's DO IT
Review and reinforcement activities

Segment 6
(6th class hour)

LEARNING LOG
Conclusion and students' self-evaluation

 **#Sentence Quiz Exercise**

The section *Exercise > Sentence Quiz* in the CD-ROM enhances learning by stimulating multiple senses as well as providing immediate feedback on students' performance.

The Sentence Quiz exercise comprises four levels.

- Level 1 – Warm-up Quiz (Look, Listen, and Type): Chinese text, *pinyin*, and audio prompts are provided.

- Level 2 – Visual-aid Quiz: Only Chinese text is provided. There are no *pinyin* or audio prompts.

- Level 3 – Audio-aid Quiz: Only audio prompts are provided.

- Level 4 – Character-selection Quiz: Only Chinese text is provided. After entering the correct *pinyin*, students are required to select the correct character from a list of similar-looking characters.

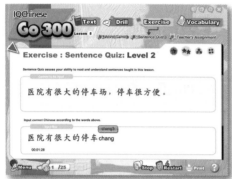

Typing practice for important sentences in every lesson reinforces the connection between words and sounds, and helps students to identify words better.

Summary Report immediately reveals students' accuracy rate and speed of typing per minute.

Detail Report lists characters typed erroneously three times during the quiz. It also shows details of errors based on categories such as *pinyin*, tone, and word selection. The instant feedback feature enables students to start on self-improvement right away.

Classroom Setup and Equipment

For small classes (up to 5 students), the teacher can show the CD-ROM features on one computer with students gathered around the screen. For large groups, a projector will be needed to project the computer's display onto a large screen so that the entire class can see.

If the classroom is not equipped with computers, the teacher may have students bring their own portable computers to class so that they can work individually or in small groups of 2 to 3 on the CD-ROM activities during designated class hours. CD-ROM activities may also be assigned as homework.

Suggestions for Teachers

We recommend that teachers

- spend 4-5 hours on each lesson in the Textbook and 2 hours on each lesson in the CD-ROM. The course materials and lesson length may be adjusted according to students' proficiency level and learning ability.

- allocate 1-2 class hours to go over with students the Review units in the Workbook as a way to check on the students' progress.

- have students complete 1-2 pages of the Workbook after every two class sessions.

- encourage students to spend 10 minutes a day on the Sentence Quiz in the CD-ROM. Practice makes perfect!

For detailed chapter-by-chapter lesson plans, teaching slides, and supplementary assignments, please refer to one of the following websites:

Cengage Learning http://www.cengageasia.com

IQChinese http://www.iqchinese.com

Scope & Sequence

Lesson	Communicative Goals	Vocabulary	Language Usage	Cultural Information
我的家人 My Family **1**	• Be familiar with the terms of address of my family members and relatives • Introduce my family members and relatives and describe our relationships	**Terms of address of family members and relatives** 爷爷, 奶奶, 伯伯, 叔叔, 姑姑, 堂哥, 堂妹, 表姐, 表弟, 外公, 外婆, 舅舅, 姨妈, 表哥, 表妹, 孙子, 外孙, 一家人, 外孙女, 女儿, 儿子, 男, 孙女, 同...	• **Usage of "都是" and "就是"** 哥哥、弟弟和我都是爸妈的儿子。 爸爸的爸爸就是我的爷爷。 • **Sentence pattern "是……，也是……"** 他是我的中文老师，也是哥哥的中文老师。 • **Usage of "同 / 一样"** 我们看同一本书。 我们看一样的书。 • **Chinese radicals "女" and "言"**	• Differences in paternal and maternal terms of address stemmed from favoritism of males in ancient, agriculture-based China. • Chinese terms of address are an expression of respect for the elders.
学校活动 School Activities **2**	• State my extra-curricular activities • Express which extra-curricular activities I would like to participate in • Use conjunction "可是" to convey a particular tone or to indicate a contrast in meaning	**Participating in school activities** 学校, 上课, 下课, 乐队, 球队, 课外活动, 参加, 回家, 想, 休息, 可是, 得 (děi), 送, 给...	• **Usage of "要 / 想"** 我要去上学。 我想去上学。 • **Usage of "得 (děi)"** 我在学校得上课，还得参加课外活动。 • **Usage of conjunction "可是"** 我想休息，可是功课还没做。 • **Sentence patterns "送…… / 送了……给……"** 爷爷送奶奶一台电脑。 爷爷送了一台电脑给奶奶。 • **Usage of Chinese punctuation "：" and "" ""** 表妹说："昨天奶奶送了一个背包给我。"	
用心做好 Try Your Best **3**	• Explain the importance of trying one's best in what he does • State if one is able or unable to complete a certain task • Use adjectives in the superlative	**Grades and examinations** 作业, 坏, 交, 大考, 小考, 完, 成绩, 重要, 用心, 最, 考, 时候, 得 (de)...	• **Sentence patterns "Verb + 不完 / Verb + 完了"** 桌上的饭菜很多，我吃不完。 桌上的饭菜我都吃完了。 • **Usage of adverbial "最"** 小明写的字最好看。 • **Turning adjectives into questions** 重要 → 重不重要? • **Sentence pattern "什么时候……? "** 我什么时候来接你? • **Chinese radical "心"**	

Lesson	Communicative Goals	Vocabulary	Language Usage	Cultural Information
我生病了 I Am Sick **4**	• Describe my symptoms to the doctor • Inquire after someone else, or inquire about the cause of a condition • Describe actions	**Sickness and recovery** 流鼻水/流鼻涕, 咳嗽, 医生, 药, 水, 鼻水, 流, 咳, 难过, 生病, 怎么, 出来, 出去…	• **Usage of "得"** 表妹咳嗽咳得真难过。 • **Sentence pattern "不……，不会……"** 不吃药，病不会好。 • **Sentence patterns "怎么了？/ 怎么……？"** 你怎么了？ 你怎么没写作业？ • **Usage of "出来 / 出去"** 弟弟生病，鼻水从鼻子流出来了。 妈妈每天早上都出去买菜。	• How traditional Chinese physicians examine their patients • Evolution of Chinese characters—pictographic characters and associative compounds
家在哪里? Where Is Your Home? **5**	• Ask for directions to a particular destination • Give directions to a particular location • Describe the location of a place	**Description of the locations of common facilities** 饭馆, 市场, 停车场, 医院, 图书馆, 球场, 向, 左转, 向前, 附近, 方便, 对面, 住, 停车, 买菜, 离, 近, 看病, 右转…	• **Usage of "有 / 在"** 我家后面有图书馆。 图书馆在我家后面。 • **Sentence pattern "……在哪里？"** 请问市场在哪里？ • **Sentence pattern "从……到……" (location)** 从我家到市场要走十五分钟。 • **Sentence pattern "去 (somewhere)(do something)"** 我去图书馆看书。 • **Linking prepositions of location and their usage** 九百个上下。 八百五十个左右。	• The traditional folklore, *The Three Moves of Mencius' Mother* • The common use of "东" (east), "西" (west), "南" (south), and "北" (north) in giving directions in some Chinese cities
我的心情 My Moods **6**	• Express my emotions and moods • Explain the cause of or reason for something	**Description of emotions and moods** 开心, 心情, 难过, 生气, 吵架, 打架, 美丽, 难看, 骂人, 自己, 带, 因为, 所以, 为什么…	• **Usage of "自己"** 我自己会做饭、洗衣服。 • **Sentence pattern "因为……，所以……"** 因为我生病了，所以我没去上学。 • **Usage of "为什么"** 你为什么心情不好？ 为什么你心情不好？ 你心情不好，为什么？ • **Positions of Chinese radicals**	• Concealment of ill feelings is a cultural expectation of Chinese to maintain social harmony.
我看球赛 Watching a Ball Game **7**	• Express my feelings when watching a ball game • Describe the results of a ball game • Make comparisons between two subjects	**Description of the happenings and feelings during a ball game** 棒球, 篮球, 兵乓球, 桌球, 比赛, ……队, 赢, 输, 精彩, 球赛, 紧张, 比, 分, 喜欢, 场, 运动, 票…	• **Usage of "比"** 十比七，红队赢，蓝队输。 我比表弟大两岁。 • **Usage of "比一比"** 我们来比一比，看谁打得好。 • **Chinese character "青"**	• A display of chivalry and sportsmanship by noblemen was often seen in Archery competitions in ancient China.

Lesson	Communicative Goals	Vocabulary	Language Usage	Cultural Information
我的爱好 My Hobbies **8**	• Talk about my hobbies • Ask about others' hobbies • Use time adverbials to indicate frequency • Describe two simultaneous actions in the same sentence	**Description of hobbies** 唱歌, 跳舞, 音乐, 跑步, 爱好, 常常, 朋友, 次, 一边……, 一边……, 每次, 小时…	• **Usage of time adverbial "常常"** 表妹喜欢跳舞，她常常参加跳舞比赛。 • **Sentence pattern "一边……，一边……"** 姐姐一边走路，一边唱歌。 • **Expansion of phrases** 上课 → 上什么课? • **Characters with more than one form of pronunciation** 好: 很好(hǎo) 　　爱好(hào)	
电视节目 Television Programs **9**	• Talk about my favorite television programs • Ask about others' favorite television programs • Express one's compliance with another person's decision or action • Express the sequence of occurrence between two actions or events	**Categories of television programs** 电视(机), 节目表, 新闻, 卡通, 电影, 打开, 节目, 加, 英文, 选, 久, 种…	• **Usage of "很久 / 太久"** 我找了很久，还是找不到图书馆。 弟弟电视看得太久了，所以作业还没写完。 • **Usage of "就" (where the second clause replicates the first clause)** 你看哪个节目，我就看哪个节目。 • **Usage of "再"** 看完电影，再去图书馆。 • **Homophones** shì: 是, 事, 市, 视	• The similar pronunciation of "书" (book) and "输" (to lose) makes books an unlucky gift for some Chinese because they believe the gift will cause a loss of something.
今天天气 The Weather Today **10**	• Describe the weather • Describe feelings of hot and cold • Describe an ongoing action or two actions that are occurring concurrently	**Description of the weather** 太阳, 阳光, 刮风, 下雨, 晴天, 阴天, 热, 冷, 着, 笑, 张著, 树, 外面…	• **Usage of "着"** 姑姑听着音乐跳舞。 • **Sentence pattern "……怎么样?"** 今天天气怎么样? • **Usage of "会 + adjective"** 明天会很热吗? 我想明天会很热。 • **Hypothetical sentences with "如果 / 要是" (if) omitted** 明天天气好，我们就去打球。 • **Usage of chinese punctuation "；"** 明天出太阳，我们就去球场打球；下雨，我们就在家里玩游戏。	

Table of Contents

我的家人
My Family

My Goals

1 Be familiar with the terms of address of my family members and relatives
2 Understand the differences between the paternal and maternal family in the Chinese society
3 Be able to introduce my family members and relatives and describe our relationships
4 Understand how radicals can classify Chinese characters into various semantic categories

yé ye
爷爷

nǎi nai
奶奶

bó bo
伯伯

bó mǔ*
伯母*

爸爸

gū fù*
姑父*

gū gu
姑姑

shū shu
叔叔

shěn shen
婶婶*

táng gē
堂哥

táng mèi
堂妹

biǎo mèi
表妹

你好！我是谢小明，他们是我的家人。

我

妹妹

*伯母 aunt
(wife of father's older brother)

*姑父 uncle
(husband of father's sister)

*婶婶 aunt
(wife of father's younger brother)

New Words

yé ye
爷爷 grandfather (paternal)

nǎi nai
奶奶 grandmother (paternal)

bó bo
伯伯 uncle (father's older brother)

shū shu
叔叔 uncle (father's younger brother)

gū gu
姑姑 aunt (father's sister)

táng gē
堂哥 older cousin (male, paternal)

táng mèi
堂妹 younger cousin (female, maternal)

biǎo mèi
表妹 younger cousin (female, both paternal & maternal)

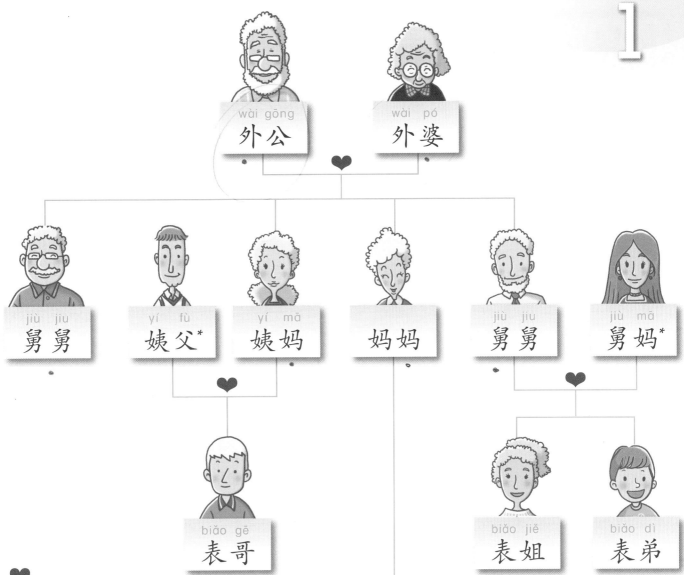

Work It Out

1 Apart from "爸爸", "妈妈", "哥哥", "姐姐", "弟弟", and "妹妹", which other relatives do you have?

2 On your computer, create your family tree and insert the Chinese terms of address of all your relatives. E-mail your teacher or print out the family tree.

*姨父 uncle (husband of mother's sister)

*舅妈 aunt (wife of mother's brother)

New Words

wài gōng 外公 grandfather (maternal)	wài pó 外婆 grandmother (maternal)	jiù jiu 舅舅 uncle (mother's brother)	yí mā 姨妈 aunt (mother's sister)
bião gē 表哥 older cousin (male, both paternal & maternal)	bião jiě 表姐 older cousin (female, both paternal & maternal)	bião dì 表弟 younger cousin (male, both paternal & maternal)	

yé ye nǎi nai ài sūn zi
爷爷奶奶爱孙子，

wài gōng wài pó ài wài sūn
外公外婆爱外孙，

sūn zi wài sūn dou shuo
孙子外孙都是我，

da jia dou shi yì jiā rén
大家都是一家人。

New Words

sūn zi
孙子 grandson
(son's son)

wài sūn
外孙 grandson
(daughter's son)

yì jiā rén
一家人 the whole family

TIP

"外" connotes something "external" and "distant". In traditional Chinese societies, when a girl gets married, she is no longer considered part of her family as she will take on her husband's surname. Her children are then known as "外孙" and "外孙女" to her parents, and her children address their maternal grandparents as "外公" and "外婆". Today, Chinese women do not necessarily take on their husband's surname upon marriage, but the maternal terms of address remain unchanged.

Why are your father's brothers differentiated by the terms "伯伯" and "叔叔" while your mother's brothers are known simply as "舅舅"?

Historically, China depended largely on agriculture, which required a lot of labor. Hence, Chinese families favored males as they could provide the manual labor on the farms. This has led to the patriarchal Chinese society we see today where the paternal terms of address are more elaborate and detailed.

Let's Learn GRAMMAR

都是

哥哥、弟弟和我都是爸妈的儿子。
我家除了妈妈，都是男的。
chu le = apart from …
妈妈和姨妈都是外公的女儿。

New Words

儿子 son

男 male

女儿 daughter

孙女 granddaughter (son's daughter)

外孙女 granddaughter (daughter's daughter)

就是

爸爸的爸爸就是我的爷爷。
妈妈的妈妈就是我的外婆。

is   also is

是……，也是……

他是我的中文老师，也是哥哥的中文老师。
我是爸爸的女儿，也是奶奶的孙女。
我是妈妈的女儿，也是外公的外孙女。

同 / 一样
tóng

我和堂哥同姓，我们都姓谢。
táng gē tóng

我的奶奶和堂妹的奶奶是同一个人。
nǎi nai   táng mèi   nǎi nai   tóng

我们看同一本书。
tóng

我们看一样的书。

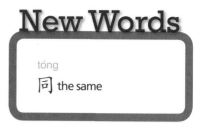

New Words

| tóng |
| 同 the same |

Think and Answer

Check the box next to the sentence that accurately describes the quantity of bread as depicted in each picture.

① 小明和大关吃同一个面包。
tóng

他们吃 → ☐ 一个面包
       → ☐ 两个面包

② 小明和大关吃一样的面包。

他们吃 → ☐ 一个面包
       → ☐ 两个面包

Go 300

WANT TO LEARN MORE?

Check out the Text > Sentence Pattern section in the Go300 CD.

Find a partner and practice the following dialogues.

⭐Task 1

Ⓐ ： 昨天你和谁一起打球？

Ⓑ ： 我表弟。
<small>biǎo dì</small>

Ⓐ ： 他是你叔叔的儿子吗？
<small>shū shu ér zi</small>

Ⓑ ： 不是。他是我舅舅的儿子，也是我的同学。
<small>jiù jiu ér zi</small>

⭐Task 2

Ⓐ ： 我堂哥大我两岁，堂妹小我一岁。
<small>táng gē táng mèi</small>

你有堂哥、堂妹吗？
<small>táng gē táng mèi</small>

Ⓑ ： 我有堂哥，没有堂妹。
<small>táng gē táng mèi</small>

我堂哥也大我两岁。
<small>táng gē</small>

Ⓐ ： 我们的堂哥一样大，
<small>táng gē</small>

都是十五岁。

TIP

"大我两岁"
means someone is two
years older than I;
"小我一岁" means
someone is one year
younger than I.

TIP

The Chinese are very respectful towards their elders and do not address them by their names. Instead they address them by the proper terms of address, even including the rank of their elders in terms of the seniority among his or her siblings (二伯, 三姑).

Because China covers a vast land, terms of address may vary slightly across different regions. For example, one's father's sisters may be known as "姑姑" in one region and "姑妈" in another. One's mother's sisters may be called "姨妈", "姨", or "阿姨" according to the norm in different regions.

★ Task 3

Ⓐ : _____

Ⓑ : 我有三个姑姑，
我叫她们大姑姑、
二姑姑和小姑姑。

★ Task 4

Ⓐ : 爸爸的爸爸就是我的爷爷。
我和爷爷同姓，我们都姓谢。

Ⓑ : 你堂哥也姓谢吗？

Ⓐ : 对，我们同姓。堂哥和我都是爷爷的孙子。

The following dialogues are adapted from the Text > Dialogue section in your  Go 300 . Listen to the CD before reading the transcript on this page.

⭐ Task 5

Ⓐ ：你的堂弟、堂妹多大了？
_{táng dì　táng mèi}

Ⓑ ：我的堂弟今年十二岁，堂妹今年十岁。
_{táng dì　　　　　táng mèi}

⭐ Task 6

Ⓐ ：你的爷爷、奶奶有几个孙子、孙女？
_{yé ye　nǎi nai　　　sūn zi　sūn nǚ}

Ⓑ ：我的爷爷、奶奶有四个孙子、两个孙女。
_{yé ye　nǎi nai　　　sūn zi　　　sūn nǚ}

⭐ Task 7

Ⓐ ：你和谁一起去外公、
_{wài gōng}
外婆家？
_{wài pó}

Ⓑ ：我和表哥、表姐一起去。
_{biǎo gē　biǎo jiě}

Ⓐ ：你的外公、外婆都在家吗？
_{wài gōng　wài pó}

Ⓑ ：是，他们都在家。

⭐ Extend Dialogues

Work in pairs and take turns to extend the dialogues in tasks 5 to 7. If you were A, which of the questions below would you select to continue each dialogue? If you were B, how would you answer the final question in each dialogue?

(1) 你爷爷的孙女和你同姓吗？

(2) 你在外公、外婆家玩什么游戏？

(3) 你的堂弟比堂妹大几岁？

Let's Learn RADICAL

A big difference between English words and Chinese characters is that while English words are made up of letters of the alphabet, Chinese characters are composed of radicals and individual components. Each radical carries a certain attribute or meaning. So we can deduce the meaning of a character by looking at its semantic association indicated by its radicals. This lesson introduces the radicals "女" and "言".

The radical "女" is typically related to femininity. The character "女" looks just like a female kneeling on the ground with both hands crossed in front of her.

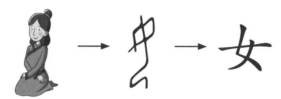

The radical "言" is commonly associated with speech. In ancient times before the writing system was established, people used to draw a mouth with curved lines radiating from it to signify sound waves. This has evolved to the earliest form of the character "言". When "言" serves as a radical in the left component, it changes its form as follows: 说

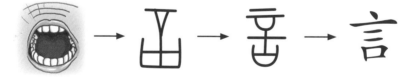

Text 1 Go 300

Read the following text carefully.

yé ye 爷爷今年八十六岁，nǎi nai 奶奶今年八十二岁，

他们有七个sūn zi孙子、两个sūn nǚ孙女、

三个wài sūn外孙和一个wài sūn nǚ外孙女。

yé ye nǎi nai 爷爷奶奶说他们很幸福，

他们能吃、能喝、能听、能看、能走，

可以天天和我们zài yì qǐ在一起*，这就是幸福。

* 在一起 stay together

Answer these questions in Chinese.

1 By how many years is Grandfather older than Grandmother?

2 How many children do the grandparents have in total?

3 Why do the grandparents feel very fortunate?

4 Does the author have a "姑姑"? How can you tell?

Read the following text carefully.

我爷爷胖胖的、矮矮的。

他爱吃面，不爱吃面包。

爷爷很能干，他会说中文，有时他教我说中文；

他会开车，有时他送我去上学。

> "会" here indicates the capability of a person who has gone through some training or practice.

爷爷有一个儿子、一个女儿、两个孙女和三个外孙。我们常常*一起吃饭，一起出去玩。

爷爷今年八十岁了，他会用电脑写电子邮件*，还会玩电脑游戏。我爱我的爷爷，我的爷爷也爱我。

*常常 often
*电子邮件 e-mail

Answer these questions in Chinese.

1. How many sons, daughters, grandsons, and granddaughters does the author's grandfather have respectively?

2. If the author is 15 years old, how much younger is he than his grandfather?

3. According to the description in the text, which of the following statements is <u>incorrect</u>?

   ☐ The author dosen't have an uncle.

   ☐ The author has an aunt.

   ☐ The author is a female.

WANT TO LEARN MORE?

Check out the Text > Reading section in the Go300 CD.

Study the family tree below and answer the questions on the following page.

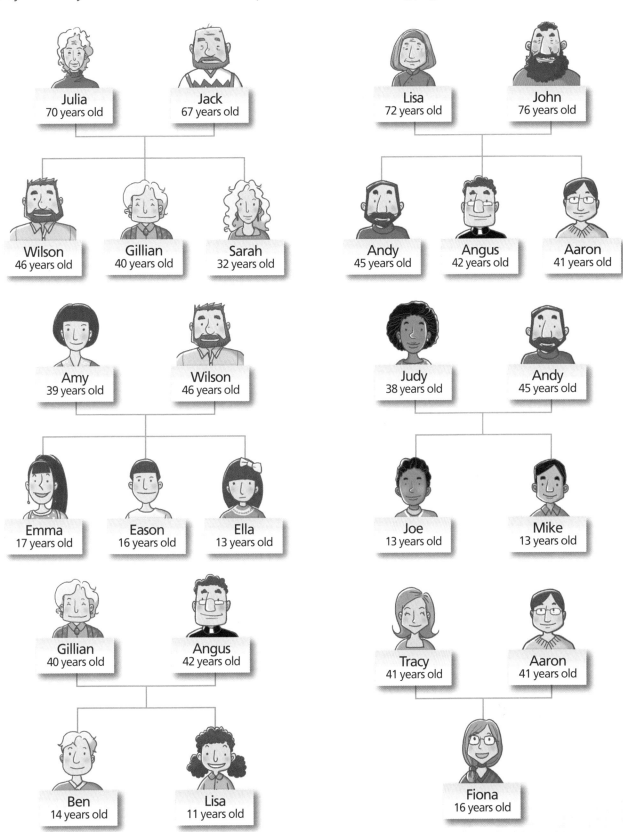

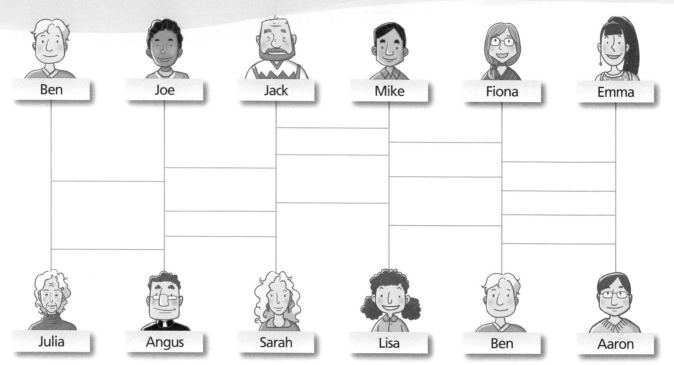

1 According to the diagram above, start with a character in the bottom row and trace the line from this character upwards, turning at <u>every</u> fork you encounter. You will be able to link the character to another character in the top row. For example, Julia will be connected to Ben.

2 State the relationship between the two characters by looking at the family tree on the previous page.

   For example, "Julia 是 Ben 的外婆wài pó。"

3 From the six pairs of characters formed, select three pairs and record their relationships in Chinese in the blanks below.

①	
②	
③	

2

学校活动
School Activities

My Goals

1 Become familiar with the names of extra-curricular activities in school
2 Be able to express which extra-curricular activity I can or would like to participate in
3 Be able to use conjunction "可是" to convey a particular tone or to indicate a contrast in meaning
4 Become familiar with Chinese punctuation " ： " and " " " " "
5 Become familiar with vocabulary associated with participating in school activities

xué xiào
学校

shàng kè
上课

xià kè
下课

yuè duì
乐队

qiú duì
球队

lā lā duì
拉拉队
(cheerleading)

qí yì shè
棋艺社
(chess club)

hé chàng tuán
合唱团
(choir)

xué shēng huì
学生会
(student union)

Work It Out

1 What extra-curricular activities have you participated in this year? What made you take part in these activities? What other extra-curricular activities would you like to engage in?

2 Imagine you are a reporter. Using after-class hours, interview three of your classmates. Ask them what their extra-curricular activities are and why they choose to participate in them. Record your interviews using any recording device.

New Words

xué xiào	shàng kè	xià kè	yuè duì	qiú duì
学校 school	上课 go to class	下课 end of class	乐队 music band	球队 ball team

Let's CHANT Go 300

<pre>
xué xiào kè wài huó dòng
学校课外活动多，
cān jiā yuè duì
参加乐队还打球，
xià kè huí jiā xiǎng xiū xi
下课回家想休息，
kě shì děi
可是还得做功课。
</pre>

New Words

kè wài huó dòng 课外活动 extra-curricular activity	cān jiā 参加 join; participate in	huí jiā 回家 go home	xiǎng 想 want
xiū xi 休息 rest	kě shì 可是 but, however	děi 得 have to	

Let's Learn GRAMMAR

TIP

"要" indicates the intention to actually do something. "想" indicates a consideration or a wish to do something. In a sentence, what follows "要" or "想" is the action that has not yet been fulfilled. Semantically, "要" is more forceful than "想" as the actual fulfillment of the action that occurs after "要" is more certain.

要 / 想
xiǎng

我要去上学。

cān jiā kè wài huó dòng
我要参加课外活动。

xiū xi
我要休息。

xiǎng
我想去上学。

xiǎng cān jiā kè wài huó dòng
我想参加课外活动。

xiǎng xiū xi
我想休息。

得
děi

děi
我得做好功课再去玩。

děi
爸爸得上班赚钱。

děi
弟弟得去上学。

TIP

When "得" is pronounced děi, what follows the word (得) has to be an action that should or must be done.

xué xiào děi shàng kè děi cān jiā kè wài huó dòng
我在学校得上课，还得参加课外活动。

děi děi
今天我得扫落叶，还得教弟弟做功课。

可是 _{kě shì}

我想休息，可是功课还没做。
（xiǎng xiū xi / kě shì）

他想吃三明治，可是没有钱。
（xiǎng / kě shì）

小明想买这本书，可是书太贵了。
（xiǎng / kě shì）

爷爷	送 _{sòng}	奶奶	一台电脑。

姑姑送表弟一双鞋。
（sòng）

叔叔送堂哥一张桌子。
（sòng）

Want More Practice?

Fit the sentences on the left into the other sentence structure ("送了⋯⋯给⋯⋯" or "送") and practice reading them.

爷爷	送了 _{sòng}	一台电脑	给 _{gěi}	奶奶。

表哥送了一支笔给表妹。
（sòng / gěi）

外公送了一本书给外婆。
（sòng / gěi）

New Words

送 _{sòng} give (as a present)

给 _{gěi} give

Go300

WANT TO LEARN MORE?

Check out the Text > Sentence Pattern section in the Go300 CD.

Let's TALK

Find a partner and practice the following dialogues.

Task 1

外公的生日 (birthday) 到了，你想送外公什么？

我想送他一张贺卡 (card)。你想送什么？

我也想送一张贺卡给他。

你想在贺卡上写什么？

_____。

Task 2

你参加什么学校活动？

我参加了乐队，你参加什么？

我参加了球队。

除了乐队，我也想参加球队。

Task 3

Ⓐ : 明天早上你来我家玩，好不好？

Ⓑ : 我很想去，可是明天早上我得上中文课。
xiǎng kě shì děi

Ⓐ : 明天下午我们一起去打球，好不好？

Ⓑ : 我很想去，可是我参加了球队，下午我得在
xiǎng kě shì cān jiā qiú duì děi
学校打球。
xué xiào

Ⓐ : 我也想参加球队。参加了球队，我们就可以
xiǎng cān jiā qiú duì cān jiā qiú duì
一起打球了。

Task 4

Ⓐ : 你们学校有什么课外活动？
xué xiào kè wài huó dòng

Ⓑ : _____。

Ⓐ : 你参加什么课外活动？
cān jiā kè wài huó dòng

Ⓑ : _____。

The following dialogues are adapted from the Text > Dialogue section in your  Go 300 . Listen to the CD before reading the transcript on this page.

⭐ Task 5

Ⓐ ： 这个星期天你有什么活动？
　huó dòng

Ⓑ ： 星期天下午，我要和同学一起去打球。

⭐ Task 6

Ⓐ ： 你参加什么课外活动？
　cān jiā　　kè wài huó dòng

Ⓑ ： 我参加了乐队，还有球队。
　cān jiā　yuè duì　　qiú duì

⭐ Task 7

Ⓐ ： 我们要去打球，你想不想一起去？
　　　　　　　　　xiǎng　xiǎng

Ⓑ ： 我想去，可是功课太多，不能去。
　xiǎng　kě shì

⭐ Task 8

Ⓐ ： 你舅舅星期六上班吗？

Ⓑ ： 不上班，他星期六在家休息。
　　　　　　　　　　　xiū xi

Let's Learn
PUNCTUATION

mào hào
： 冒号
(colon)

When a colon is placed after a name or a term of address, what follows is usually the speech of that person. When it is placed after a collective phrase, what follows is commonly an elaboration or explanation of that collective phrase.

The colon can also be used together with quotation marks (" "). Placed after words such as "说" or "问 ", they contain the content of one's speech or question.

小明：你妈妈在家吗？

大关：不在，她去上班了。

cān jiā   xué xiào huó dòng   qiú duì   yuè duì
我参加了两个学校活动：球队和乐队。

sòng   gěi
表妹说："昨天奶奶送了一个背包给我。"

yǐn hào
" " 引号
(quotation marks)

Quotation marks can be used together with the colon to draw out the content of what a person is saying or asking. If there is an emphasis in a sentence, quotation marks can also be used to focus the reader's attention on the key point.

nǚ
"妈"和"姑"这两个字都有"女"，妈妈和姑姑都

nǚ
是女 (female) 的。

Practice It

Fill in the blanks with the correct punctuation marks.

xiǎng xiū xi
① 小明问 ☐☐ 你想休息吗 ☐☐

② ☐ 说 ☐ 和 ☐ 课 ☐ 这两个字都有 ☐ 言 ☐☐

Read the following text carefully.

_{kè wài huó dòng}
课外活动我都爱，

_{yuè duì}
星期一、星期三和星期五，有乐队，

星期二和星期四，要打球，

_{xià kè huí jiā xiǎng xiū xi}
下课回家想休息，

妈妈叫我做功课，

奶奶叫我写中文，

从早到晚忙忙忙，真辛苦。

Answer these questions in Chinese.

1 On which days does the author <u>not</u> have ball practice?
On which days does the author <u>not</u> have band practice?

2 What does the author wish to do when he gets home?

3 Who wants the author to practice writing Chinese
when he gets home?

 Text 2

Read the following text carefully.

在学校，除了要上课，还有很多活动。有乐
队、球队、拉拉队，还有学生会。

星期六、星期日不用上课，可是我和小明都
很忙。我们参加一样的课外活动：乐队和球队。

我和小明一起上课，一起参加活动。每一个 *
活动都好玩，每一个活动我们都爱。

*每一个 each one of

Answer these questions in Chinese.

1 What extra-curricular activities does the author participate in?

2 On which days do the author and 小明 engage in their extra-curricular activities?

3 Does the author enjoy being in the music band and on the ball team? How can you tell?

4 Does the author think that a student's life is hectic? As a student, are you busy? Why?

Go300

WANT TO LEARN MORE?

Check out the Text > Reading section in the Go300 CD.

Let's DO IT

The societies in school are recruiting members.

Mary, Julie, and Lily wish to join the same society. The following table shows you the schedule of their present extra-curricular activities. Study it, and with the help of the posters provided, complete the conversation below.

	星期日	星期一	星期二	星期三	星期四	星期五	星期六
Mary			中文课		电脑课		
Julie				xué shēng huì 学生会		hé chàng tuán 合唱团	
Lilly	中文课					hé chàng tuán 合唱团	

Julie ： 我要参加拉拉队，你们想和我一起参加吗？
　　　　 (cān jiā lā lā duì) ... (cān jiā)

Mary ： ＿＿＿＿＿＿＿＿＿＿＿＿＿＿＿＿＿＿＿ 。 （可是） kě shì

Lilly ： ＿＿＿＿＿＿＿＿＿＿＿＿＿＿＿＿＿＿＿ 。 （可是） kě shì

＿＿＿＿＿＿＿＿＿＿＿＿＿＿＿＿＿＿＿ 。 （一起）

LEARNING LOG

I can...

	Excellent	Good	Fair	Needs Improvement

1 state the names of common extra-curricular activities. ☐ ☐ ☐ ☐

2 use "想" to express my desires. ☐ ☐ ☐ ☐

3 use "可是" to convey a particular tone or to indicate a contrast in meaning. ☐ ☐ ☐ ☐

4 list the reasons for participating in certain extra-curricular activities. ☐ ☐ ☐ ☐

5 use the colon (：) to introduce the contents of a speech or an explanation, and use the quotation marks (" ") to contain the contents of a speech or to emphasize certain words and phrases. ☐ ☐ ☐ ☐

6 write "校", "活", "动", "想", and "给". ☐ ☐ ☐ ☐

用心做好
Try Your Best

1 Be able to explain the importance of trying one's best in what he does
2 Be able to express if one is able or unable to complete a certain task
3 Be able to use adjectives in the superlative
4 Become familiar with the radical "心" (heart)
5 Become familiar with vocabulary associated with classes, examinations, and grades

kǎo shì
考试
(examination)

kǎo juàn
考卷
(test paper)

chéng jì dān
成绩单
(school report card)

zuò yè
写作业
(do homework)

bào gào
报告
(report)

New Words

zuò yè
作业 homework

huài
坏 bad

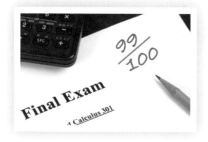

好

huài
坏/不好

Play It

Form two teams and send a representative per team to the blackboard. The teacher will randomly recite three words from this page. Each representative is to pick out the placards on the blackboard that contain the words and arrange them in the order which they were recited. The first team to complete the task wins.

jiāo zuò yè
上课还要交作业，

dà kǎo xiǎo kǎo　　wán
大考小考忙不完，

chéng jì　　huài　zhòng yào
成绩好坏不重要，

yòng xīn　　　zuì zhòng yào
用心做好最重要。

Think About It

Do you think grades matter? Do your parents share your view?

Are grades crucial to gaining entry into a school? What other criteria will schools consider in entry applications? Why do you think these criteria matter?

Think about it and ask around — what do your classmates think about grades?

New Words

jiāo	dà kǎo	xiǎo kǎo	wán
交 hand in	大考 final examination	小考 quiz	完 finished

chéng jì	zhòng yào	yòng xīn	zuì
成绩 grades	重要 important	用心 pay attention	最 most

Let's Learn GRAMMAR

Verb + 不完 (wán) / Verb + 完 (wán) 了

学校大考 (dà kǎo)、小考 (xiǎo kǎo) 多，我忙不完 (wán)。

桌上饭菜很多，我吃不完 (wán)。

星期五我就考完 (kǎo wán) 了。

桌上的饭菜我都吃完 (wán) 了。

最 (zuì)

最小 (zuì)　　　　最大 (zuì)

小明写的字最 (zuì) 好看。

我有五个杯子，这个杯子最 (zuì) 大。

哥哥、弟弟和我，弟弟的成绩 (chéng jì) 最 (zuì) 好。

TIP
When comparing three or more subjects, you should use "最 + adjective" to express the adjective in the superlative (the highest or lowest degree).

Turning Adjectives into Questions
AB ➤ A 不 AB ?

zhòng yào
重要 ➤ chéng jì zhòng zhòng yào 学校成绩重不重要？

yòng xīn
用心 ➤ yòng yòng xīn 你上课用不用心？

好看 ➤ 这本书好不好看？

TIP
When an adjective composed of two characters (AB) is in the predicate of a sentence, it can be written in the form "A不 AB" to change the sentence into a positive–negative question. To answer such a question, you just need to state if you agree with the adjective used on the subject of the question.
For example:
Question: 这本书好不好看？
Answer: 这本书很好看。(Positive)
这本书不好看。(Negative)

shí hou
什么时候……？

Ⓐ : shí hou 我什么时候来接你？

Ⓑ : 请你下午五点半来接我。

Ⓐ : shí hou 你什么时候不用上课？

Ⓑ : 我星期六和星期日不用上课。

New Words

shí hou
时候 time

WANT TO LEARN MORE?

Check out the Text > Sentence Pattern section in the Go300 CD.

用心做好 31

Find a partner and practice the following dialogues.

⭐ Task 1

Ⓐ : 明天要交作业，你的作业写完了吗？

Ⓑ : 作业又多又难(difficult)，我写不完。

Ⓐ : 你什么时候要写作业？

你不会的作业，我可以教你。

Ⓑ : 谢谢，下午三点半请你教我写作业。

⭐ Task 2

Ⓐ : 你前天的考试重不重要？

Ⓑ : 前天的考试是大考，很重要。

Ⓐ : 谁考得最好？

Ⓑ : 小明考得最好。小明上课很用心，

老师说上课用心，就能考得好。

New Words

得 de (a particle used after a verb or an adjective to express possibility or capability)

用心做好

A ： 哥哥，这盒 (carton) 牛奶可以喝吗？
_hé_   _kě yǐ_

B ： 你看看上面的日期 (date)。
_rì qī_

A ： 上面写~~十二月二日~~，

可是今天是~~十一月六日~~。

牛奶 <u>坏了</u> (坏了 / 没坏) 了，
huài   _huài_

<u>不可以</u> (可以 / 不可以) 喝。

Task 4

A ： 你小考考得好不好？
xiǎo kǎo kǎo de

B ： 我考得不好。
kǎo de

> "会" here indicates the possibility of a certain outcome.

A ： 考得不好，你妈妈会生气 (angry) 吗？
kǎo de   _shēng qì_

B ： 妈妈说成绩好坏不重要，用心做好最重要。
chéng jì huài zhòng yào yòng xīn zuì zhòng yào

**Task 5**

Complete the dialogues below according to the pictures. When you have done that, listen to the dialogues in the Text > Dialogue section in your [Go 300] to compare your answers.

①

六月				18	25
星期日		4	11	19	26
星期一		5	12 大考	20	27
星期二		6	13 大考	21	28
星期三		7	14 大考	22	29
星期四	1	8	15 大考	23	30
星期五	2	9	16	24	
星期六	3	10	17		

A ： 你们学校什么时候
shí hou
大考？
dà kǎo

B ： _____

②

A ： 我交作业了，
jiāo zuò yè
你交了没有？
jiāo

B ： _____

③

A ： 你考得好不好？
kǎo de

B ： _____

④

A ： 小明的成绩好不好？
chéng jì

B ： _____

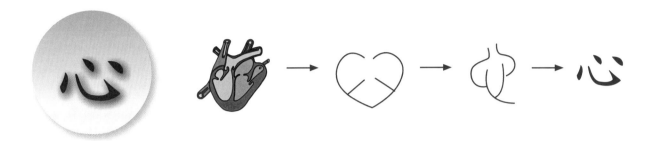

"心" is a common radical in Chinese characters. The character "心" originated from the illustration of the heart. As a radical, "心" appears in two forms: ⎡忄⎤ in the left-right combination and ⎡心⎤ in the top-bottom combination. When placed as a radical in the top-bottom combination, "心" remains unchanged in its form. However, when placed as a radical in the left-right combination, it changes from its original form into "忄", just like the case of "打" and "拿" as we have learnt earlier.

Most characters with the radical "心" are semantically related to the heart. The two characters below are both made up of a combination of the radical "心" and the component "亡", but their meanings are different. The following examples also illustrate how you can use the "Break Down Character" technique to remember these two characters.

"亡" means "nothing" or "to perish". Imagine "忙" as the heart being so busy that it is always standing up, with no time to rest.

忙 → 很忙 → 我从早到晚都很忙。

Imagine "忘" as the heart sitting down for a rest, and many things are forgotten as a result.

忘 → 忘了 → 我忘了今天要大考。
dà kǎo

用心做好

Let's READ

Read the following text carefully.

用心学，成绩就会好，
(yòng xīn, chéng jì)

我开心*，爸妈也开心。
(kāi xīn, kāi xīn)

不用心，成绩就不好，
(yòng xīn, chéng jì)

我不开心，大家都不开心。
(kāi xīn, kāi xīn)

用心学，小心做，样样*学得好，
(yòng xīn, yàng yàng de)

样样做得好，样样成绩都会好。
(yàng yàng de, yàng yàng chéng jì)

* 开心 happy
* 样样 everything

Answer these questions in Chinese.

1 What will one achieve when he pays attention?

2 What must one do in order to do well?

3 Fill in the blanks below with "用心", "小心", and "开心".

(a) 妈妈，_____！前面有车子。

(b) 上课_____，大考_____，成绩好，就很_____。

Text 2

Read the following text carefully.

老师说："上课要用心^{yòng xīn}。"

哥哥说："做功课要用心^{yòng xīn}，

参加活动要用心^{yòng xīn}，玩游戏也要用心^{yòng xīn}。"

我问爸爸："什么是用心^{yòng xīn}？"

爸爸说："做一件^{jiàn}*事，多听、多问、多想，这

就是用心^{yòng xīn}。"

做每一件^{jiàn}事，做得^{de}好坏^{huài}不重要，用心^{yòng xīn}去做最重要^{zuì zhòng yào}。

*件 (a measure word for abstract concepts, matters, documents, clothing, etc.)

Answer these questions in Chinese.

1 What does it mean by "用心"?

2 According to the passage, when should one pay attention?

3 Apart from what was mentioned in the text, how do you think one can pay attention?

Go300

WANT TO LEARN MORE?

Check out the Text > Reading section in the Go300 CD.

 **Reading Aloud**

The teacher will decide to use the texts from this lesson's **Let's Read** or **Let's Chant** for this activity.

1 Get into small teams. Each team has to memorize the text allocated by the teacher, and choreograph actions and group formations to accompany the recital of the text.

2 Each team will take turns to perform. The rest of the teams will grade the performing team on <u>a total score of five</u> with the score sheet provided below.

3 When all teams have performed their recitals, each team will comment on each of the other teams' strengths and give its score for that team. The winning team is the team with the highest total score.

	Team 1	Team 2	Team 3	Team 4
Diction				
Oral Presentation				
Choreography				
Total score				

Record of each team's strengths

LEARNING LOG

I can...

		Excellent	Good	Fair	Needs Improvement
1	state what is important in preparing for an examination.	☐	☐	☐	☐
2	use "最" to express adjectives in the superlative.	☐	☐	☐	☐
3	use "Verb +完了" and "Verb +不完" appropriately in sentences.	☐	☐	☐	☐
4	explain the meaning of the radical "心", and identify the different forms of it in various characters.	☐	☐	☐	☐
5	write "考", "完", "作", "交", and "最".	☐	☐	☐	☐

我生病了
I Am Sick

My
Goals

1   Be able to convey in simple terms the symptoms of my sickness to my doctor
2   Be able to inquire after someone else, or to inquire about the cause of a condition
3   Be able to describe actions
4   Understand how some Chinese characters evolved from illustrations
5   Become familiar with vocabulary associated with being sick

Get Started

liú bí shuǐ
流鼻水 /

liú bí tì
流鼻涕

ké sou
咳嗽

⭐ **Play It**

1 With your teacher, decide on accompanying actions for the vocabulary on this page.

2 Stand in three rows and number yourselves in each row according to the order of your positions.

3 The teacher will recite a series of words and phrases. The first student in each row will perform the action of the first word or phrase, the second student will perform the action for the second, and so on.

4 A wrong action or forgetting to perform an action will disqualify the student and he will have to sit down. The row with the most number of students still standing wins.

dù zi tòng
肚子痛
(stomachache)

fā shāo
发烧
(fever)

yá tòng
牙痛
(toothache)

yī shēng
医生

hù shi
护士
(nurse)

bìng rén
病人
(patient)

chī yào
吃药
(take medicine)

hē shuǐ
喝水
(drink water)

New Words

liú bí shuǐ liú bí tì	ké sou	yī shēng	yào	shuǐ
流鼻水/流鼻涕 running nose	咳嗽 cough	医生 doctor	药 medicine	水 water

Let's CHANT Go300

bí shuǐ bí shuǐ liú
鼻水鼻水流不停，

ké sou ké   nán guò
咳嗽咳得真难过。

yī shēng   yào
看医生，要吃药，

shēng bìng
生病在家多休息。

TIP Traditional Chinese physicians examine their patients differently from the way modern doctors do with their stethoscope. Apart from asking the patients to describe their condition, traditional Chinese physicians also check and rely on the patients' appearance, breath, and pulse to determine their diagnoses. Today, these traditional methods are still practiced by many traditional Chinese physicians in the world.

The picture on page 39 shows a Chinese physician taking the pulse of a patient.

New Words

bí shuǐ 鼻水 mucus	liú 流 flow
ké 咳 cough	nán guò 难过 miserable
shēng bìng 生病 sick	

我生病了

Let's Learn GRAMMAR

表妹咳嗽 ké sou	咳 ké	得	真难过 nán guò 。

堂哥走路走得真快(fast) kuài 。

爸爸扫落叶扫得真辛苦。

外公学电脑学得真好。

不	吃药 yào ，	病	不会	好 。

不看医生 yī shēng ，你的咳嗽 ké sou 不会好。

不用心 yong xin，你的成绩 chunzing 不会好 hui 。

TIP

"得" has three forms of pronunciation, each with a different meaning. When speaking, one must articulate the word well so that the listener will not be confused.

得 děi : have to
你咳嗽了，得多喝水。
(You are coughing and have to drink more water.)

得 de : a particle used after a verb or an adjective to express possibility or capability
谁考得最好?
(Who attained the best score?)

得 dé : get / obtain
我得到100块钱。
(I obtained 100 dollars.)

出来 chū lái

弟弟生病 shēng bìng ，鼻水 bí shuǐ 从
鼻子 bí zi (nose)流出来 liú chu lai 了。

妹妹说："姐姐，请你出来 chū lái ，
有人找你。"

怎么了？ / 怎么……？
zěn me zěn me

你怎么了？
zěn me

小明今天没来上学，他怎么了？
zěn me

弟弟怎么了，今天都没说话(speak)？
zěn me shuō huà

你怎么没写作业？
zěn me

你怎么在流鼻水？
zěn me liú bí shuǐ

奶奶怎么回家？
zěn me

这个问题怎么回答？
zěn me

New Words

怎么 how
zěn me

出来 come out
chū lái

出去 go out
chū qù

Go300

WANT TO LEARN MORE?

Check out the Text > Sentence Pattern section in the Go300 CD.

出去
chū qù

妈妈每天早上都出去
chū qù
买菜(buy vegetables or groceries)。
mǎi cài

爸爸，我们出去打球了。
chū qù

Find a partner and practice the following dialogues.

⭐Task 1

A : 你怎么了，眼睛红红的？

B : 我的眼睛好痒(itchy)，痒得真难过。

A : 你得去看医生。

B : 看了，我今天早上去看医生了。

A : 医生说什么？

B : 医生要我多休息。

> "要" here means "to ask somebody to do something".

⭐Task 2

A : 今天天气很好，你怎么不出来打球？

B : 我生病了，不能出去。

A : 你得去看医生，吃了药，多休息，病就会好。

B : 药很难吃(tastes awful)，我不想吃药。

A : 不吃药，病不会好的。

Task 3

Think About It

What do you do if you catch a cold? When do you decide to see the doctor? Why?

A： 你怎么了？
_{zěn me}

B： 我又流鼻水，又咳嗽。
_{liú bí shuǐ} _{ké sou}

A： 你咳嗽咳了几天了？
_{ké sou ké} _{qǐ}

B： 三天了。我咳嗽咳得很难过。
_{ké sou ké de} _{nán guò}

A： 你鼻水流了几天了？
_{bí shuǐ liú} _{wǒ}

B： 三天了。我鼻水也流个不停。
_{bí shuǐ} _{liú}

A： 你吃一点儿药，多休息，就会好的。
_{diǎn} _{yào} _{xiang}

B： 这个药怎么吃？
_{zhè ge} _{yào zěn me}

A： 每天吃完饭，就要吃药。
_{měi tian} _{wan fan} _{yào}

我生病了 45

Task 4

Can you identify pairs of dialogue from the eight utterances below? Organize them into four dialogues and fill in the following table. When this is done, you may listen to the Text > Dialogue section in your 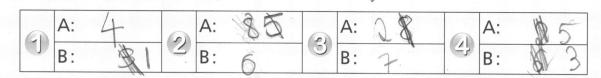 for the correct answers.

	①		②		③		④
A:	4	A:	~~8~~5	A:	2~~8~~	A:	~~8~~5
B:	~~8~~1	B:	6	B:	7	B:	~~8~~3

nán guò
① 他考得不好，很难过。

yī shēng
② 他看医生了吗？

shēng bìng
③ 他生病了，不能来上课。

zěn me
④ 他怎么了？

zěn me
⑤ 他怎么没来上课？

ké sou　　　　liú bí shuǐ　　　　　yī shēng
⑥ 除了咳嗽，我还流鼻水，我要去看医生。

yī shēng
⑦ 看了，医生要他多休息。

ké sou
⑧ 你咳嗽吗？

Let's Learn CHARACTER

⭐ Origin of Chinese Characters

Some Chinese characters originated directly from pictorial illustrations of objects and hence are known as "象形字" (xiàng xíng zì) (pictographic characters). Some other Chinese characters are composed of two or more components, each with a meaning of its own, to form a new character. The meaning of the new character is easily decipherable from its components and such characters are thus known as "会意字" (huì yì zì) (associative compounds). Look at the examples below. Can you tell what character each of the following illustrations has evolved into? Write it down.

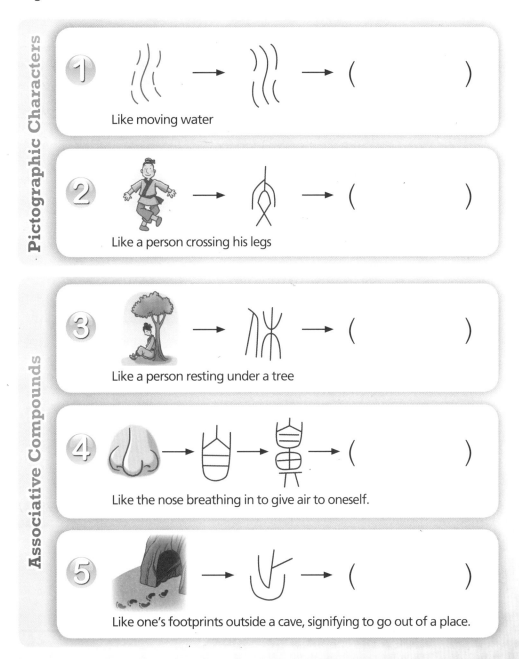

Pictographic Characters

① Like moving water → ( )

② Like a person crossing his legs → ( )

Associative Compounds

③ Like a person resting under a tree → ( )

④ Like the nose breathing in to give air to oneself. → ( )

⑤ Like one's footprints outside a cave, signifying to go out of a place. → ( )

Read the following text carefully.

shēng bìng　　　　　ké sou ké　　　tíng　　　bí shuǐ　　yě liú　　　shēng
我生病了，咳嗽咳个不停，鼻水也流个不停。生

bìng　nán guò　　　　　xiǎng　　　　　　xiǎng yào
病很难过，我不想吃饭，也不想吃药。可是妈妈说：

kě　　　　　　　　　　yě　　　kě　　　　yào　　　　　　yào
不可以不吃饭，也不可以不吃药；不吃饭，不吃药，

bìng jiù
病就不会好。

> "吃饭" here does not merely refer to eating rice, but a full meal. Rice is the staple food for the Chinese, and so it is very apt to use "吃饭" to convey the idea of eating a full meal.

yī shēng　　　shēng bìng　　　　　　　　　　　　shēng bìng
医生说：生病要多休息。爷爷说：生病要多喝
shuǐ　　　　　shēng bìng　　　chū qù　　　　　　　　xiū xi
水。爸爸说：生病不要出去玩，要多休息。

Answer these questions in Chinese.

1 What symptoms does the author display?　咳嗽　流鼻水

2 What does the author's mother say he must eat when he is sick?

3 According to the author's family and doctor, what are the things that one should and should <u>not</u> do when he is sick? Write them down in the table below.

Things to do when one is sick	Things <u>not</u> to do when one is sick
喝水	不吃饭 不吃药

Read the following text carefully.

shēng bìng
每个人都会生病，

shēng bìng   nán guò
生病很难过：

不能玩，不能上学，

不能参加活动。

shēng bìng   yī shēng
生病了，要看医生，

tīng yī shēng de huà
要听医生的话*。

> Here, "就" carries an hypothetical tone. It indicates that the desired outcome can be achieved as long as the conditions stated in the preceding clause are met.

bìng
病好了，就可以玩；

bìng
病好了，就可以上学；

bìng
病好了，就可以参加活动。

*听医生的话 obey the doctor's instructions

Answer these questions in Chinese.

1 Who will fall sick?

2 What do we do when we fall sick?

3 What can we do once we are well?

Go 300

WANT TO LEARN MORE?

Check out the Text > Reading section in the Go300 CD.

流鼻水 liú bí shuǐ　咳嗽 ké sou　发烧 fā shāo　牙痛 yá tòng

dù zi tòng
肚子痛

jiǎo tòng
脚痛
(leg pain)

Let's DO IT

1 Obtain two dice and pair up with a friend to play the roles of a doctor and a patient. The student acting as the patient will roll the dice simultaneously to determine the two symptoms of illness.

2 Match the numbers on the dice to the symptoms numbered on this page and carry out the following dialogue. If both dice yield the same number, the student acting as the doctor will say "你没有生病，多休息就好了。".

医生：你怎么了？
yī shēng　zěn me

病人：我又流鼻水，又咳嗽，很难过。
bìng rén　liú bí shuǐ　ké sou　nán guò

医生：你除了要吃药，还要多喝水。
yī shēng　yào　shuǐ

吃了药，多喝水，病就会好。
yào　shuǐ　bìng

LEARNING LOG

I can...

		Excellent	Good	Fair	Needs Improvement
1	state simple symptoms of sicknesses such as cough and running nose in Chinese.	☐	☐	☐	☐
2	use "怎么了？" to inquire after somebody else.	☐	☐	☐	☐
3	pronounce "得" appropriately, and use "Verb + 得 + Adjective" to describe an action.	☐	☐	☐	☐
4	identify "水" and "交" as pictographic characters.	☐	☐	☐	☐
5	identify "休", "鼻", and "出" as associative compounds.	☐	☐	☐	☐
6	write "水", "流", "难", "过", and "病".	☐	☐	☐	☐

5

家在哪里?
Where Is Your Home?

My Goals

1 Be able to ask for directions to a particular destination
2 Be able to give directions to a particular location
3 Be able to describe the facilities surrounding a particular area
4 Become familiar with prepositions of location that look similar
5 Become familiar with the names of common facilities around my house

Get Started

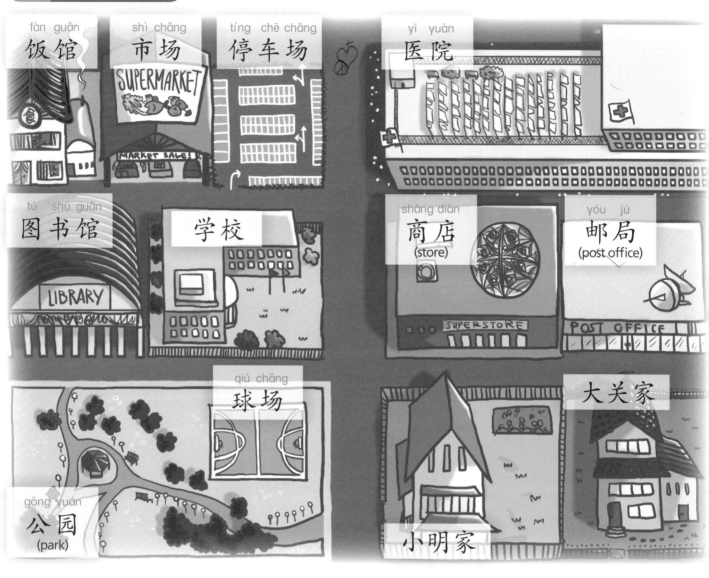

fàn guǎn 饭馆	shì chǎng 市场 (SUPERMARKET)
tíng chē chǎng 停车场	yī yuàn 医院
tú shū guǎn 图书馆 (LIBRARY)	学校
	shāng diàn 商店 (store)
	yóu jú 邮局 (post office)
qiú chǎng 球场	大关家
gōng yuán 公园 (park)	小明家

xiàng zuǒ zhuǎn
向左转
(turn left)
left

xiàng qián zǒu
向前走
(go ahead)

xiàng yòu zhuǎn
向右转
(turn right)
right

New Words

fàn guǎn 饭馆 restaurant	shì chǎng 市场 market
tíng chē chǎng 停车场 parking lot	yī yuàn 医院 hospital
tú shū guǎn 图书馆 library	qiú chǎng 球场 court for ball games (basketball, tennis, etc.)

Mark the Route

Listen carefully to your teacher and trace out the route on the map according to your teacher's directions.

52 家在哪里?

 **Let's CHANT** Go 300

for open ground we say 'chang'

with roof = guan

gong 公 public

xiàng zuǒ zhuǎn　　　tú shū guǎn

向左转，图书馆。

xiàng qián　　　　　yī yuàn

向前走，是医院。

　　　　　shì chǎng　　fù jìn

学校、市场在附近，

　　　　　　　　fāng biàn

做什么，都方便。

TIP

mèng mǔ sān qiān

The Three Moves of Mencius' Mother (孟母三迁) is a traditional Chinese folklore which goes like this:

mèng zǐ

Mencius (孟子) was a great philosopher in ancient China, and one of the main followers of Confucius' ideas. Mencius did not like to study at all when he was a little boy. His mother strongly believed that the environment a child lived in was crucial to his development. Hence, she relocated their home from beside a cemetery to the side of a marketplace, and finally to a vicinity near a school.

If you could decide on a location to reside in, what would be the biggest consideration in your decision?

New Words

xiàng	zuǒ zhuǎn	xiàng qián	fù jìn	fāng biàn
向 to	左转 turn left	向前 forward	附近 nearby	方便 convenient

Let's Learn GRAMMAR

我家 后面 *hòu miàn* 有 图书馆 *tú shū guǎn*。

学校附近 *fù jìn* 有停车场 *tíng chē chǎng*。

我家对面 *duì miàn* 有市场 *shì chǎng*。

图书馆 *tú shū guǎn* 在 我家 后面。

停车场 *tíng chē chǎng* 在学校附近 *fù jìn*。

市场 *shì chǎng* 在我家对面 *duì miàn*。

New Words

对面 *duì miàn* opposite

住 *zhù* live

TIP "哪里" and "什么" are both interrogative pronouns. "哪里" is used to ask about a location. When answering such a question, you simply need to replace "哪里" with your answer without having to change the structure of the sentence.

……在哪里?

Ⓐ： 请问市场 *shì chǎng* 在哪里?

Ⓑ： 市场 *shì chǎng* 在我家附近 *fù jìn*。

Ⓐ： 请问你住 *zhù* 在哪里?

Ⓑ： 我住 *zhù* 在图书馆 *tú shū guǎn* 后面。

TIP

"到" in the sentence structure "从……到……" is a preposition which means "up to". However, "到" in the sentence "走路十分种就到了。" is a verb which means "to reach" or "to arrive at". In Examples 3 to 5, the speaker is aware of the travelling time between the two locations. To express the opinion that it does not take very long to travel to the destination, one can use the phrase "time + 就到了".

从……到…… (location)

shì chǎng
从我家到市场要走十五分钟。

qiú chǎng   xiǎo shí
从学校到球场要走半个小时(hour)。

shì chǎng
从我家到市场，走十五分钟就到了。

qiú chǎng   xiǎo shí
从学校到球场，走半个小时就到了。

tú shū guǎn   yī yuàn
从图书馆到医院，开车二十分钟就到了。

            tú shū guǎn
我 去 图书馆 看书。

tíng chē chǎng tíng chē
姑姑去停车场停车。

shì chǎng mǎi cài
外婆去市场买菜。

New Words

tíng chē
停车 park (a vehicle)

mǎi cài
买菜 buy vegetables or groceries

Go300

WANT TO LEARN MORE?

Check out the Text > Sentence Pattern section in the Go300 CD.

Let's TALK

Find a partner and practice the following dialogues.

New Words

离 lí be away from

近 jìn close, near

看病 kàn bìng see a doctor

Task 1

Ⓐ : 学校离你家近吗？

Ⓑ : 很近，学校就在我家对面。

opposite (duì miàn)

Ⓐ : 除了学校，你家附近还有什么？

Ⓑ : 我家附近还有图书馆、球场和饭馆。

Ⓐ : 你家附近什么都有，真方便。

Task 2

Ⓐ : 你家附近有医院吗？

Ⓑ : 有。从我家到医院，开车十分钟就到了。
奶奶去医院看病很方便。

Ⓐ : 你家附近有市场吗？

Ⓑ : 我家附近没有市场。从我家到最近的市场要
走四十五分钟，我们得开车去买菜。

⭐Task 3

A : 请问去图书馆怎么走？
tú shū guǎn

B : 向前走，走到路口 (intersection) 向左转，
xiàng qián lù kǒu xiàng zuǒ zhuǎn

就可以到图书馆了。
tú shū guǎn

A : 请问从图书馆到球场怎么走？
tú shū guǎn qiú chǎng

B : 从图书馆出来，向右转，
tú shū guǎn xiàng yòu zhuǎn

就可以到球场了。
qiú chǎng

New Words

右转 turn right
yòu zhuǎn

⭐Task 4

A : 我的笔坏了，学校
附近有卖 (sell) 笔的商
fù jìn mài shāng
店吗？
diàn

B : 有，学校附近有卖
fù jìn mài
笔的商店。
shāng diàn

A : 在学校的左边，

还是右边？

B : 在学校对面。
duì miàn

Paper, gunpowder, printing compass

TIP

Apart from "向左转" (turn left) and "向右转" (turn right), there are some regions in northern China such as Beijing where people commonly use "东" (east), "西" (west),
dōng xī
"南" (south), and "北" (north) in giving directions. Intensive city planning in these cities since ancient times has given rise to neat and perpendicular roads, rendering it very convenient to give directions using the four
nán běi
cardinal directions (东西南北).
dōng xī nán běi

The compass, which is very useful in helping us find directions, is one of China's four main inventions. Even before the magnetic compass was invented, China had already invented a cart that worked on a gear system and always pointed south to help people find their directions.

The following dialogues are adapted from the Text > Dialogue section in your  Go 300 . Listen to the CD before reading the transcript on this page.

⭐Task 5

Ⓐ : 你住在哪里？
zhù

Ⓑ : 我住在学校附近。
zhù fù jìn

Ⓐ : 你家附近有什么？
fù jìn

Ⓑ : 我家附近有学校、图书馆，还有市场。
fù jìn tú shū guǎn shì chǎng

⭐Task 6

Ⓐ : 我晚上给你打电话，方便吗？
fāng biàn

Ⓑ : 不要太晚，十点以后我就
不可以接电话(answer phone) 了。
jiē diàn huà

⭐Task 7

Ⓐ : 怎么去你家？

Ⓑ : 从学校出来向左转，走十分钟就到了。
xiàng zuǒ zhuǎn

Let's Learn CHARACTER

⭐ Linking Prepositions of Location

"上", "下", "左", and "右" are words that specifically describe a position. However, when they are placed together, the specificity decreases. For example, when paired together, "上下" mean "approximately", and "上上下下" means "everywhere".

Ⓐ 你的学校有多少人？

Ⓑ 九百个上下。 — means "about 900 people"

Ⓒ 八百五十个左右。 — means "about 850 people"

我要找王医生，可是医院上上下下都找不到他。

⭐ Prepositions of Location that Look Similar

Some characters look very similar. Hence we have to be very careful when writing such characters so they will be differentiated. How can we remember the differentiation between these characters? Here, disassembling a character to its components is a good way to help us remember these characters, as illustrated by the example of "卡" below.

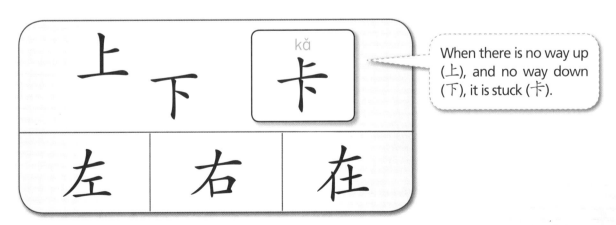

When there is no way up (上), and no way down (下), it is stuck (卡).

Let's READ

Text 1 Go 300

Read the following text carefully.

我家前面有一个小学*，
我走五分钟就到了；
我家后面有一个市场，
妈妈买菜很方便；
我家左边有一个医院，
奶奶可以走路去看病；
图书馆也在我家附近，
我们都爱去那里*看书。

* 小学 elementary school
* 那里 there

Answer these questions in Chinese.

1　What facility is on the left of the author's house?

2　Where is the marketplace in relation to the author's house?

3　What are the facilities in the vicinity of the author's house?

Text 2

Read the following text carefully.

去年八月，我们一家人去了
上海*看*舅舅。
shàng hǎi kàn

到了上海，爸爸问我们："怎么去舅舅家？"
shàng hǎi

姐姐说："我们可以看地图*。"
dì tú

哥哥说："我可以用电脑找到舅舅家。"

弟弟说："我们可以请舅舅来接我们。"弟弟
说完，我们就看到舅舅来接我们了。

我们在上海住了两天，我们去了图书馆看书，
shàng hǎi   tú shū guǎn
还去了市场买菜。上海是一个很大的城市*，也是一
shì chǎng mǎi cài   shàng hǎi   chéng shì
个很好玩的城市。
chéng shì

*上海 Shanghai   *看 visit   *地图 map   *城市 city

Answer these questions in Chinese.

1   Where did the author go during his school break in August?

2   The author's siblings suggested a few ways to get to their uncle's house. What are they? Do you have any other suggestions?

3   Which places did the author visit when he was in Shanghai?

How can I get there?

1. Pair up and obtain a dice. Take turns to role-play A and B.

2. Toss the dice twice—the first one is to determine A's present location and the second is to determine his next destination.

3. Refer to the map on page 52 of this book and carry out the dialogue below. The words in red may be replaced accordingly.

túshūguǎn
图书馆

shìchǎng
市场

qiúchǎng
球场

学校

 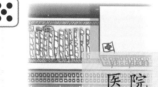
医院

小明家

Ⓐ 我在球场，请问去市场怎么走？
　　　qiú chǎng　　　　　　　shì chǎng

Ⓑ 从球场出来，向右转，到了路口向左转，看到停车场
　　qiú chǎng　　　xiàng yòu zhuǎn　　lù kǒu xiàng zuǒ zhuǎn　　tíng chē chǎng
　　向左转，就可以到市场了。
　　xiàng zuǒ zhuǎn　　　　　shì chǎng

LEARNING LOG

I can...

		Excellent	Good	Fair	Needs Improvement
1	ask for directions using "⋯⋯在哪里？" and "去⋯⋯怎么走？".	☐	☐	☐	☐
2	give directions to a location in the neighborhood, and estimate the time needed to get there.	☐	☐	☐	☐
3	describe the facilities in the vicinity of an area.	☐	☐	☐	☐
4	understand the meaning when prepositions of location are paired or grouped together such as "上下", "左右", and "上上下下".	☐	☐	☐	☐
5	write "住", "向", "转", "图", and "馆".	☐	☐	☐	☐

6

我的心情
My Moods

My Goals

1 Express my emotions and moods
2 Explain the cause of or reason for something
3 Recognize that radicals may appear in various positions in different characters
4 Become familiar with vocabulary associated with emotions and moods

kāi xīn

开心

xiào

笑
(laugh)

nán guò

难过

hài pà

害怕
(scared)

kū

哭
(cry)

chǎo jià

吵架

dǎ jià

打架

shēng qì

生气

New Words

kāi xīn 开心 happy	nán guò 难过 sad	chǎo jià 吵架 quarrel	dǎ jià 打架 fight	shēng qì 生气 angry

Go 300

xīn qíng　　　　　　　　　měi lì
心情好，看人看花都美丽，

xīn qíng 〈Kai hua〉
心情坏，看人看花都难看。
　　　　ren　hua　nán kàn

chǎo jià mà rén
吵架骂人没有用，
　　　　　yong ✓ flower
　　　　　✓ useful

zì　jǐ shēng qì　you nán guò
自己生气又难过。
　　　　　　you　yong
有用 = useful

我很帅

Shuài
帅 handsome

New Words

xīn qíng	měi lì	nán kàn	mà rén	zì jǐ
心情 mood	美丽 beautiful	难看 terrible, ugly	骂人 scold	自己 self

Let's Learn GRAMMAR

TIP The phrase "自己" (self) refers to the subject of each clause.

zì jǐ
自己

zì jǐ
我自己会做饭，会洗衣服。

"自己" in this sentence refers to "me".

zì jǐ de yào zì jǐ
自己的作业要自己写。

"自己" in this sentence has no particular reference; it refers to anybody who hears this sentence.

dài dǎ qiú chū zì jǐ
哥哥不带弟弟去打球，弟弟就自己去了。

"自己" in this sentence refers to "弟弟".

---

yīn wèi   suǒ yǐ
因为 我生病了，   所以 我没去上学。

yīn wèi   dǎ jià   suǒ yǐ   mà
因为堂哥和同学打架，所以叔叔骂他。

(A): wèi shén me xīn qíng
你们为什么心情不好？

(B): yīn wèi   zhǎo zhǎo
因为我找不到我要的书，
suǒ yǐ   xīn qíng
所以我心情不好。

(C): xīn qíng   yīn wèi   nan
我心情不好，因为我不能
Can jia chiu dui
参加球队。   zhǎo
找 = Look for

TIP "因为……，所以……" is a sentence structure that expresses cause and effect. The phrase after "因为" conveys the cause and the phrase after "所以" conveys the effect. When the effect is positioned at the beginning of the sentence, the word "所以" may be omitted, leaving "因为" to introduce the cause in the second clause.

New Words

dài	yīn wèi	suǒ yǐ	wèi shén me
带 bring	因为 because	所以 so	为什么 why, what for

你　为什么　心情不好？
wèi shén me　xīn qíng

她为什么考得不好？
wèi shén me

他为什么不来打球？
wèi shén me

为什么　你　心情不好？
wèi shén me　xīn qíng

为什么她考得不好？
wèi shén me

为什么他不来打球？
wèi shén me

你　心情不好，　为什么？
xīn qíng　wèi shén me

她考得不好，为什么？
wèi shén me

他不来打球，为什么？
wèi shén me

TIP

The question tag "为什么" may be used to ask for a reason or a motive. It can be positioned before or after the subject, or at the end of the question.

Questions with "为什么" can often be answered with the "因为……，所以……" sentence structure.

"为什么 + 不" is often a question in retort, indicating that the speaker feels the situation should have been feasible or possible.

WANT TO LEARN MORE?

Check out the Text > Sentence Pattern section in the Go300 CD.

Find a partner and practice the following dialogues.

⭐ Task 1

A : 你会和同学吵架吗？
   chǎo jià

B : 我们很少 (seldom) 吵架，因为吵架没有用。
   hěn shǎo   *chǎo jià*   *yīn wèi chǎo jià*   *yong*

A : 你的成绩不好，你妈妈会骂你吗？
   chéng zhǐ   *mà*

ll ur test results f bad, will ur mum be angry/ unhappy/ scold.

B : 不会。妈妈说："成绩好坏不重要，
   chéng zhǐ   *Chng zi*   *huai zhi*

用心做好最重要。"
Yong   *Zui zhong*   *zui zhong yao = most important*

⭐ Task 2

zhong yao = important

A : 你怎么了？
   zhen ma le

B : 我心情不好。
   xīn qíng

A : 为什么？
   wèi shén me

B : 因为我吃了哥哥的面包，哥哥很生气。
   yīn wèi   *chi*   *shēng qì*

A : 你对哥哥说对不起，再买一个面包给他，
   dui bu zhi   *mai yi ge*   *mian bao*

你哥哥就不会生气了。
   shēng qì

⭐ **Task 3**

Ⓐ　我看你很开心。
　　　　kāi xīn

Ⓑ　因为我心情好。
　　yīn wèi　xīn qíng

Ⓐ　为什么你心情好？
　　wèi shén me　xīn qíng

Ⓑ　因为我找到心情好的方法 (method)。
　　yīn wèi zhaO daO xīn qíng　　fāng fǎ

　　多笑心情就好，少生气心情也好。
　　xiào xīn qíng　　　shaO shēng qì xīn qíng ye

Ⓐ　所以我们要多笑，少生气。
　　suǒ yǐ　　　　　xiào　　　shēng qì

⭐ **Task 4**　♡

Ⓐ　你今天心情好吗？
　　　　xīn qíng

Ⓑ　我去打球所以我开心。 _____ ◦
　　wo qu da qiu

Ⓐ　你为什么 开心 _____ ?
　　　　wèi shén me

Ⓑ　因为我爱打球。 _____ ◦

Can you identify the pairs of dialogue from the eight utterances below? Organize them into four dialogues and fill in the following table. When this is done, you may listen to the Text > Dialogue section in your Go 300 for the correct answers and fill in the blanks.

①	A: 2 ✓	②	A: 4 ✓	③	A: 7 ✓	④	A: 8 ✓
	B: 6 ✓		B: 3 ✓		B: 1 ✓		B: 5 ✓

❶ 他们两个都要这个 <u>蓝球</u>，所以吵架了。
　　　　　　　　　　　　　　　 suǒ yǐ chǎo jià

② 你在骂谁？
nǐ zàimà shuí

❸ 我考得不好，所以很<u>不开心</u>。
　　　　　　　　suǒ yǐ

❹ 你为什么心情不好？
wèi shén me xīn qíng

❺ 外婆爱<u>花</u>，我们可以买花去看她。

❻ 我在骂弟弟，<u>他和妹妹打架</u>。
　　　　mà　　因为

❼ 他们两个在吵什么？
　　　　　　chǎo

❽ 去医院看外婆，要带什么？
qu yī yuàn　wài pó　　　dài

We have learned that radicals bear meanings and classify characters into various semantic categories. For example, a character with the radical "女" is associated with the meaning of femininity; a character with the radical "言" is related to speech. However, the position of a radical in each character varies—it may be positioned as the top, bottom, left, or right component. This lesson illustrates the different positions of some radicals.

 **Trace It**

Trace out the radical of the last character in each category using a color pencil or highlighter.

Radicals in the top component

Radicals in the bottom component

Radicals in the left component

Radicals in the right component

★ Text 1 ◎ Go 300

Read the following text carefully.

tiān
天 *，有好天气，坏天气，
　　　　xīn qíng　　　　xīn qíng
人，有好心情，坏心情。

tiān　　bu
天，不是天天好天气，
　　bu　　　　　　xīn qíng
人，不是天天好心情。

　　bu　　　zài jiā lǐ　　bu chu qù
天气不好，我在家里不出去，
xīn qíng bu　　　　jiuchu qu zou yi zou
心情不好，我就出去走一走。

明天，又是好天气，
　　　　you　　　　xīn qíng
明天，又是好心情。 天天↓
Ming　　　　　　　　　　everyday

* 天 sky

Answer these questions in Chinese.

1 What does the author do when he is in a good mood?

2 What does he do when he is in a bad mood?

3 At times, the weather may be pleasant or dreadful; moods may
   be good or bad. Are your moods influenced by the weather?

Text 2

Read the following text carefully.

姐姐和表妹要参加学校乐队，妈妈买了一样的白衣服给她们。

姐姐瘦瘦的，穿上白衣服很好看；表妹胖胖的，穿上白衣服也很好看。可是姐姐不爱自己的样子，她说自己太瘦了；表妹也不爱自己的样子，她说自己太胖了。

妈妈说："一个人胖一点儿、瘦一点儿没关系，外表*好不好看不重要，心里*美*最重要。你的心里美，大家看你都好看。"

　　　　　　　　*外表 appearance　　*心里 one's heart and mind　　*美 beautiful

Answer these questions in Chinese.

1　Why does the author's mother buy his sister and cousin a set of white outfit each?

2　Do the author's sister and cousin like how they look respectively? Why?

3　Do you think one's outward appearance and beauty are important? Why?

 **"North–South–East–West" Origami Game**

1 Prepare a square piece of paper for a game of origami.

   (1) Fold the paper in half diagonally. Fold it again in half. Open it and fold in each corner to meet at the center of the paper (see diagram ❶).

   (2) Flip the paper over on its back and fold in each corner to meet at the center of the paper (see diagram ❷).

   (3) On the side of the paper which looks like the character "田", write the four emotions ("生气", "开心", "难过", and "害怕") in the four squares (see diagram ❸).

   (4) Flip the paper over and in each triangle, write the possible reasons for the feelings reflected on the other side. Write down two reasons for each emotion (see diagram ❹).

   (5) Fold the paper into a rectangle to create a flexagon (see diagram ❺).

❶ 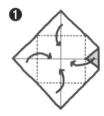 ❷ 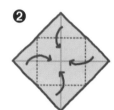 ❸ 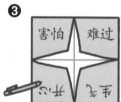 ❹ 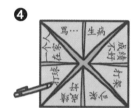 ❺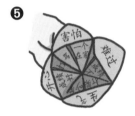

2 Find a classmate and ask him to select any of the four emotions you have written down and a number from 1 to 10. According to the number selected by your classmate, flex your flexagon vertically and then horizontally to reveal the reason for the feeling. With the sentence structure "因为···，所以···", your classmate has to read out the entire sentence. For example, "因为我大考的成绩好，所以我很开心。"

3 Play this game with five other classmates. On a separate sheet of paper, write down their sentences and obtain their signatures.

LEARNING LOG

I can...	Excellent 😄	Good 🙂	Fair 😐	Needs Improvement 🙁
1 use vocabulary associated with emotions to express my moods.	☐	☐	☐	☐
2 identify who the phrase "自己" refers to in different sentences and use it appropriately.	☐	☐	☐	☐
3 use "为什么……?" to ask for a reason, and "因为……，所以……" to give a reason.	☐	☐	☐	☐
4 recognize that radicals may appear in the top, bottom, left, or right component in different characters.	☐	☐	☐	☐
5 write "情", "美", "吵", "因", and "为".	☐	☐	☐	☐

LESSON

7

我看球赛
Watching a Ball Game

My **Goals**

1 Describe the happenings at a ball game
2 Make comparisons between two subjects
3 Understand how the pronunciation of some characters is determined by its components
4 Become familiar with vocabulary associated with ball games and the feelings associated with watching the games

bàng qiú *baseball*
棒球

lán qiú *basketball*
篮球

zú qiú *football*
足球
(soccer)

pīng pāng qiú *ping pong / table tennis*
乒乓球

wǎng qiú *tennis*
网球
(tennis)

měi shì zú qiú
美式足球
(American football)

american football

bǐ sài
比赛
contest / match / competition

win

duì yíng *team A*
A 队 赢

duì shū *loss*
B 队 输
Team B

⭐ Work It Out

1 What are the different scoring systems of ball games? How is the champion determined in various ball games?

2 What ball games have similar scoring systems?

Discuss the above questions with a friend or research on it on the Internet, and present the information in the following class.

Zhong guo dui
↓
China team

New Words

Go 300

bàng qiú　　zhuō qiú
打棒球，打桌球，

jīng cǎi qiú sài　zhǔn jǐn zhāng
精彩球赛真紧张，

qiú
你一球，我一球，

yíng　　shū méi guān xì
你赢我输没关系。

New Words

zhuō qiú
桌球 billiards

jīng cǎi
精彩 outstanding, fantastic

qiú sài
球赛 ball game

jǐn zhāng
紧张 nervous

TIP

"桌球" has different meanings in different regions. In northern China, it refers to billiards; in southern China, it refers to table tennis.

TIP

In ancient China, archery was viewed as a competition between noblemen. It was standard procedure for opponents to bow to each other before entering the competition grounds. A round of drinks and merry-making would also take place after the competition regardless of the results of the contest to show the men's chivalry and sportsmanship.

Qualities of a sportsman (respecting one's opponents, doing one's best, not gloating after a victory and not disheartened after a loss) have transcended time and remain unchanged today.

What is the most important thing to you in a competition? Have you ever lost in a competition and yet felt very satisfied and proud of yourself?

Let's Learn GRAMMAR

bǐ
比

	1	2	3	4	5	6	7	8	9	
红队	0	0	0	2	3	2	0	2	1	10
蓝队	0	0	1	2	0	2	0	0	2	7

bǐ duì yíng duì shū
十比七，红队赢，蓝队输。

duì yíng fēn duì shū fēn
红队赢了三分，蓝队输了三分。

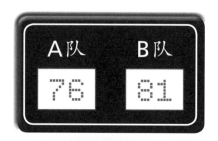

bǐ duì yíng yíng fēn
七十六比八十一，B队赢了，赢了五分。

duì yíng duì fēn
B队赢A队五分。

bǐ shū shū fēn
十一比九，大关输了，输了两分。

shū fēn
大关输小明两分。

New Words

bǐ
比 compare

fēn
分 score

| 我 | 比
bǐ | 表弟 | 大两岁。 |

哥哥比我高。
bǐ

妈妈比爸爸紧张。
bǐ　　　jǐn zhāng

奶奶比我难过。
bǐ

这本书比那本书便宜。
bǐ

小明的成绩比我的好。
bǐ

下午的球赛比上午的精彩。
qiú sài bǐ　　　　jīng cǎi

"我比表弟大两岁。"
means the same as
"我大表弟两岁。".

比一比
bǐ bǐ

我们比一比，看谁打得好。
bǐ bǐ

我们两个比一比，看谁写得好。
bǐ bǐ

小明喜欢和同学比一比，看谁考得好。
xǐ huan　　　　bǐ bǐ

New Words

喜欢 like
xǐ huan

Go300

WANT TO LEARN MORE?

Check out the Text > Sentence Pattern section in the Go300 CD.

Find a partner and practice the following dialogues.

New Words

chǎng
场 (a measure word used for a contest)

Task 1

Ⓐ : 今天我看了一场很精彩的球赛。
chǎng　jīng cǎi　　qiú sài

Ⓑ : 今天是哪一个队和哪一个队的比赛？
duì　　　　duì　　bǐ sài

Ⓐ : 今天是红队和绿队的篮球比赛。
duì　　　duì　　lán qiú bǐ sài
　　两队你一球，我一球，打得很精彩。
duì　　　　　　　　　　　jīng cǎi

Task 2

Ⓐ : 今天下午是哪一个队和哪一个队的比赛？
duì　　　　　duì　　bǐ sài

Ⓑ : 今天下午是_____和_____的比赛。
bǐ sài

Ⓐ : 哪一个队赢了？
duì yíng

Ⓑ : _____。

Ⓐ : _____队输了几分？
duì shū　　　fēn

Ⓑ : _____。

Task 3

A 你喜欢什么运动？
xǐ huan *yùn dòng*

B 我喜欢打球，我最喜欢打棒球，也喜欢看
xǐ huan *xǐ huan* *bàng qiú* *xǐ huan*
球赛。
qiú sài

A 你喜欢看哪一个队的比赛？
xǐ huan *duì* *bǐ sài*

B 我喜欢看_____队的比赛。你要不要
xǐ huan *duì* *bǐ sài*
一起去看球赛？
qiú sài

A 我想去看球赛，可是球赛的票太贵了，
qiú sài *qiú sài* *piào*

_____。

Task 4

A 明天学校要大考。

B 明天你要考什么？

A 明天我要考中文。我要和小明比一比，
bǐ *bǐ*
看谁考得好。

B 你紧张吗？
jǐn zhāng

A 我有一点儿紧张，可是我妈妈比我还紧张。
jǐn zhāng *bǐ* *jǐn zhāng*

New Words

yùn dòng	*piào*
运动 exercise	票 ticket

The following dialogues are adapted from the Text > Dialogue section in your . Listen to the CD before reading the transcript on this page.

⭐ Task 5

Ⓐ : 你要去看球赛吗？
<small>qiú sài</small>

Ⓑ : 不去，我的功课还没有做完。

⭐ Task 6

Ⓐ : 球赛一张票多少钱？
<small>qiú sài   piào</small>

Ⓑ : 一张票六十块钱，一张学生票
<small>piào   piào</small>

　　　 三十块钱。

⭐ Task 7

Ⓐ : 比赛精彩吗？哪一个球队赢了？哪一个球队输了？
<small>bǐ sài jīng cǎi   qiú duì yíng   qiú duì shū</small>

Ⓑ : 很精彩！蓝队赢了，绿队输了。
<small>jīng cǎi   duì yíng   duì shū</small>

⭐ Task 8

Ⓐ : 你喜欢打什么球？
<small>xǐ huan</small>

Ⓑ : _____

Let's Learn CHARACTER

Some characters in Chinese are made up of a single component; others are composed of a combination of different components. Some components classify characters into various semantic categories, as we have learnt of the radicals "女", "言", and "心". Some components can also determine the pronunciation of the characters they are part of. In the following lesson, we introduce a component that can determine the pronunciation of its character.

qīng

青

"青" literally means the color "green". It also connotes the meaning of "beauty" and "happiness". When "青" is part of a character, the character is often semantically associated with joyful events. The pronunciation of the characters with "青" are also similar.

Practice It

Write down the *pinyin* of the following characters.

jīng
精 → The best

qíng
晴 → Nice day

qíng
情 → Mood

qǐng
请 → please

晴

"晴" means "a fine day". This character will appear in page 112 of this book. Have a guess at pronouncing this character before checking out the correct pronunciation.

Read the following text carefully.

哥哥参加学校的球队（qiú duì），下星期六要比赛（bǐ sài），爸爸要我算一算，我们一共要买几张票（piào）？

我算一算：爷爷、奶奶、外公、外婆、姑妈*（gū mā）一家四个人、叔叔一家三个人、舅舅一家五个人、姨妈一家两个人，加上*（jiā shàng）爸爸、妈妈、姐姐，还有我，一共二十二个人，要买二十二张票（piào）。

一张票（piào）三块钱，一共多少钱？

*姑妈 aunt (father's sister)
*加上 add

Answer these questions in Chinese.

1 What tickets is the author buying?

2 How many people are there in his paternal aunt's family?

3 How many people are there in the author's family? How much will all the tickets cost?

4 Read the passage in the CD (Text > Reading: 1-2). Who in the author's family is not able to go to the game? How many tickets does the author buy eventually, and what is the total cost of the tickets?

Text 2

Read the following text carefully.

　　哥哥星期六要比 ^{bǐ sài} 赛了，妈妈比 ^{bǐ} 哥哥还紧 ^{jǐn zhāng} 张，要他多喝水，多吃水 ^{shuǐ guǒ} 果*，多休息，不要玩电脑游戏。

　　比 ^{bǐ sài} 赛那天，哥哥打得很好，可是，他们球 ^{qiú duì} 队输 ^{shū} 了，输 ^{shū} 了两分 ^{fēn} ，哥哥很难过。爸爸说："输 ^{shū} 了没关系，你打得很好。"

　　我说："哥哥打得很棒 ^{bàng} ！哥哥打得很精彩 ^{jīng cǎi} ！"我们都喜 ^{xǐ huan} 欢看他打球。

*水果 fruit　　*棒 great

Answer these questions in Chinese.

1　Who is playing in the game? Who is the most nervous about it?

2　Does Older Brother win or lose his game? How does he feel?

3　What does Father say to Older Brother after the game?

Go300

WANT TO LEARN MORE?

Check out the Text > Reading section in the Go300 CD.

Let's DO IT

Telephone Invitation To A Ball Game

1 Pair up with a partner and assume roles of A and B.

2 Obtain a dice and B tosses it twice.

3 The number from the first toss determines the ball game that B would like to watch: 1 or 2 – Table Tennis Game; 3 or 4 – Baseball Game; 5 or 6 – Soccer Game.

4 The number obtained from the second toss determines how much money B has: 1 – $10, 2 – $20, and so on.

5 Change the details of the following conversation according to the information determined from tossing the dice, bearing in mind proper phone etiquette.

Ⓐ ： 你想看球赛吗？
    qiú sài

Ⓑ ： 我喜欢看足球比赛。什么时候有足球比赛？
    xǐ huan   zú qiú bǐ sài   zú qiú bǐ sài

    一张票多少钱？
    piào

Ⓐ ： 十一月十七日有足球比赛，一张票三十五块钱。
    zú qiú bǐ sài   piào

Ⓑ ： 我有六十块钱，我可以和你一起去看。/
    票太贵了，我不能去。
    piào

LEARNING LOG

I can...

		Excellent	Good	Fair	Needs Improvement
1	name common sports such as baseball, table tennis and soccer in Chinese.	☐	☐	☐	☐
2	use sports-related vocabulary such as "○○比○○", "精彩", "输赢", and "紧张" to describe a game or one's feelings when watching a game.	☐	☐	☐	☐
3	use "比" to make a comparison.	☐	☐	☐	☐
4	recognize that characters with the component "青" are often associated with the meaning of beauty and happiness.	☐	☐	☐	☐
5	write "精", "彩", "运", "票", and "比".	☐	☐	☐	☐

我的爱好
My Hobbies

My Goals

1 Talk about my hobbies and ask others about their hobbies
2 Describe the frequency in the occurrence of an action
3 Describe two simultaneous actions in the same sentence
4 Recognize some Chinese characters with two or more forms of pronunciation
5 Become familiar with vocabulary associated with one's hobbies

chàng gē

唱歌

tiào wǔ

跳舞

yīn yuè

听音乐
(listen to music)

看书

huà huà

画画
(paint)

shū fǎ

书法
(calligraphy)

pǎo bù

跑步

liáo tiān

聊天
(chat)

diàn yǐng

看电影
(watch a movie)

⭐ Play It

1 Draw nine boxes to make up a cross-grid puzzle (see diagram below). In any order you wish, fill in each box with one of the nine words or phrases introduced on this page.

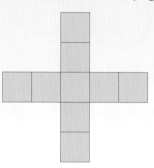

2 The teacher will recite the vocabulary in any order she wishes. Students circle the vocabulary in their cross-grid puzzle as they are read out. The first student to circle all the vocabulary in a straight line wins.

3 Alternatively, the teacher may draw lots to select a student who will read aloud a word or phrase from this page. An accurate pronunciation entitles him to circle that word or phrase in his cross-grid puzzle. A wrong pronunciation will relegate the turn to another student.

New Words

chàng gē	tiào wǔ	yīn yuè	pǎo bù
唱歌 sing a song	跳舞 dance	音乐 music	跑步 run, jog

每个人都有<ruby>爱好<rt>ài hào</rt></ruby>，

你爱打球爱运动，

她爱<ruby>唱歌<rt>chàng gē</rt></ruby>爱<ruby>跳舞<rt>tiào wǔ</rt></ruby>，

我爱看书玩电脑。

New Words

<ruby>爱好<rt>ài hào</rt></ruby> hobby

Let's Learn GRAMMAR

^{cháng cháng}
常常

^{cháng cháng} ^{péng you} ^{chàng gē}
姐姐常常和朋友一起唱歌。

^{tiào wǔ} ^{cháng cháng}
表妹喜欢跳舞，她常常参加

^{tiào wǔ}
跳舞比赛。

^{cì}
大关每个星期来我家两次，

^{cháng cháng}
他常常来找哥哥。

TIP

"很少"，"有时"，"常常"，and "每次" are time adverbials which indicate the frequency of an action or event. "每次" means "every time"; "常常" means "often"; "有时" means "sometimes"; and "很少" means "seldom". In a typical sentence structure, they are positioned before the verb phrase.

For example:
➤ 我家附近有图书馆和球场，我有时去看书，有时去打球。
➤ 小明一年去一次奶奶家，他很少去看奶奶。

^{yì biān} ^{yì biān} ^{chàng gē}
姐姐　一边　走路，　一边　唱歌。

^{yì biān} ^{yì biān}
哥哥一边看球赛，一边喝果汁。

^{yì biān} ^{yīn yuè} ^{yì biān}
妹妹一边听音乐，一边扫落叶。

^{yì biān} ^{yì biān}
妈妈一边做饭，一边打电话。

New Words

^{cháng cháng} 常常 often	^{péng you} 朋友 friend	^{cì} 次 time; instance	^{yì biān} ^{yì biān} 一边……，一边…… do the things at the same time

Expansion of Phrases
AB ➜ A_B

上课 ➜ 上什么课?

chàng gē   chàng   gē
唱歌 ➜ 唱什么歌?

tiào wǔ   tiào   wǔ
跳舞 ➜ 跳什么舞?

打球 ➜ 打什么球?

TIP Some characters may be combined to form meaningful phrases. They may even be separated in a sentence and yet retain their meaning as when they are combined.

老师上的课很有用。

chàng   gē
弟弟唱的歌很好听。

tiào   wǔ
堂哥跳的舞很好看。

měi cì
我每次都上五十分钟的课。

měi cì   xiǎo shí
哥哥每次都打一个小时的球。

měi cì   tiào   wǔ
姐姐每次都跳三十分钟的舞。

New Words

měi cì
每次 every time

xiǎo shí
小时 hour

Go 300

WANT TO LEARN MORE?

Check out the Text > Sentence Pattern section in the Go300 CD.

Find a partner and practice the following dialogues.

Task 1

Ⓐ: 你的爱好是什么？
ài hào

Ⓑ: 我喜欢听音乐。你的爱好是什么？
yīn yuè ài hào

Ⓐ: 我喜欢唱歌。你什么时候听音乐？
chàng gē yīn yuè

Ⓑ: 我常常一边写作业，一边听音乐。
cháng cháng yì biān yì biān yīn yuè

你什么时候唱歌？
chàng gē

Ⓐ: 我常常一边扫地 (sweep the floor)，
cháng cháng yì biān sǎo dì

一边唱歌。
yì biān chàng gē

Task 2

Ⓐ: 星期天你要做什么？

Ⓑ: 星期天我要去跳舞。
tiào wǔ

Ⓐ: 每次要跳几个小时？
měi cì tiào xiǎo shí

Ⓑ: 我每次都跳三个小时的舞。
měi cì tiào xiǎo shí wǔ

Ⓐ: 我也喜欢跳舞，跳舞很开心。
tiào wǔ tiào wǔ

⭐Task 3

Ⓐ : 你和朋友有一样的爱好吗？
péng you ài hào

Ⓑ : 有，我们都爱运动，我们常常一起运动。
cháng cháng

Ⓐ : 你和朋友会吵架吗？
péng you

Ⓑ : 我们很少 (seldom) 吵架，因为吵架没有用。
hěn shǎo

⭐Task 4

Ⓐ : 你喜欢运动吗？

Ⓑ : 喜欢。

Ⓐ : 你喜欢做什么运动？

Ⓑ : 我喜欢跳舞，我和妹妹明天要参加跳舞比赛。
tiào wǔ tiào wǔ

Ⓐ : 你们参加比赛紧张吗？

Ⓑ : 我不紧张，可是妹妹很紧张。

The following dialogues can be found in the Text > Dialogue section in your  Go 300 . Listen to the CD first before practicing the dialogues in pairs. The student assuming the role of B has to complete the dialogues using his own information.

⭐ Task 5

Ⓐ : 你的爱好是什么？

Ⓑ : (我喜欢听音乐，也喜欢跳舞。)

Ⓐ : 你喜欢听什么音乐？

Ⓑ : _____ 。

⭐ Task 6

Ⓐ : 你在学什么？

Ⓑ : (我在学跳舞。)

Ⓐ : 每次学几个小时？

Ⓑ : _____ 。

Let's Learn CHARACTER

Some Chinese characters have more than one form of pronunciation and the variants typically have different meanings. The following illustrates some of these words that we have learnt before.

好

hǎo 弟弟上课很用心，他的成绩很好。

hào 我的爱好是跳舞，我喜欢一边唱歌，
ài hào *tiào wǔ* *yì biān chàng gē*
一边跳舞。
yì biān tiào wǔ

便

pián 这本书三块钱，很便宜。

biàn 图书馆在我家对面，很方便。

得

de 昨天的球赛打得很精彩。

děi 我明天得上课，还得参加唱歌比赛。
chàng gē

A third way of pronouncing "得" is dé, which means "obtain or achieve".

Practice It

Fill in the *pinyin* on top of the boxed characters.

① 妹妹的 爱好 是唱歌，她唱 得 真 好听。
chàng gē *chàng*

② 从学校到我家 得 开车半个小时，很不 方便。
xiǎo shí

Let's READ

⭐ Text 1 💿 Go300

Read the following text carefully.

dòng　　　dòng
每天都要动*一动，

dòng dòng nǎo
动动脑*，看书、上学、想问题；

dòng dòng　　　　　　　　　　　　jiā shì
动动手，打球、打字、做家事*；

dòng dòng　　　　　　chàng gē
动动嘴，吃喝、唱歌、打电话；

dòng dòng jiǎo　　　　　　pǎo bù　tiào tiào wǔ
动动脚*，散步、跑步、跳跳舞。

dòng　　dòng　　dòng jiǎo
动嘴、动手又动脚，不要忘了多

dòng nǎo
动脑。

* 动 exercise; to move something
* 脑 brain
* 家事(家务) household chores
  jiā wù
* 脚 foot

Answer these questions in Chinese.

1   How do we exercise when we take a stroll, jog, or dance?

2   According to the text, what do we do when we "exercise our brain"?

3   According to the text, what do we do when we "exercise our mouth"?

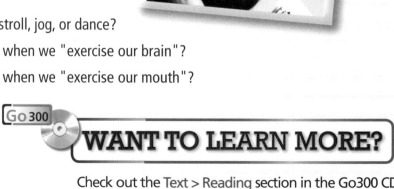

Go300 **WANT TO LEARN MORE?**

Check out the Text > Reading section in the Go300 CD.

Read the following text carefully.

每个人都有爱好，爷爷爱看书，奶奶爱散步。爸爸的爱好是和朋友聊天，妈妈的爱好是种花。

妹妹喜欢跳舞，姐姐爱买衣服，我喜欢一边听音乐，一边唱歌。

哥哥的爱好是看书，他喜欢去图书馆看很多不同的书，因为他想做医生。

妈妈说：“做自己喜欢的事，心情就会好，所以每一个人都要有自己的爱好。”

Answer these questions in Chinese.

1 What does everyone in the author's family like to do? Write down each of their hobbies in Chinese in the table below.

爷爷	奶奶	爸爸	妈妈

哥哥	姐姐	我 (the author)	妹妹

2 What is Older Brother's ambition?

3 Why should all of us have a hobby that we enjoy?

Let's DO IT

1. Obtain a blank piece of paper and a rubber band. Fold the paper into eight equal parts and cut out eight identical strips of paper. Stack the eight strips of paper together, fold them in the middle and secure the middle with the rubber band to create a booklet (See diagram ❶ and ❷).

2. Write down "1. 爱好" on the front cover, and "2. 去哪里？" on the back cover. Flip the booklet onto the reverse side so that its middle pages now become the front and back covers. Write down "3. 和什么人？" on this front cover and "4. 常去吗？" on this back cover (See diagram ❸ and ❹).

3. In every page in the booklet, write down the possible answers to the prompts provided on the cover pages. For example, (1) 跳舞；(2) 学校；(3) 朋友；(4) 常常.

4. Get five friends for this activity. Draw lots to choose the phrases from the booklet and practice the dialogues with Ⓐ 's questions as provided below. Ⓑ should answers accordingly and in complete sentences.

Ⓐ: 你的爱好是什么？
ài hào

Ⓐ: 你去哪里跳舞？
tiào wǔ

Ⓐ: 你和谁一起去学校跳舞？
tiào wǔ

Ⓐ: 你常常和朋友一起去学校跳舞吗？
cháng cháng *péng you* *tiào wǔ*

LEARNING LOG

I can...	Excellent	Good	Fair	Needs Improvement
1 talk about my hobbies and ask about others' hobbies.	☐	☐	☐	☐
2 use "常常" appropriately in sentences to indicate the frequency of an action or event.	☐	☐	☐	☐
3 use "一边……，一边……" appropriately in sentences to indicate that two actions or events are occurring concurrently.	☐	☐	☐	☐
4 recognize the different forms of pronunciation of "好", "便", and "得".	☐	☐	☐	☐
5 write "唱", "歌", "朋", "友", and "常".	☐	☐	☐	☐

电视节目
Television Programs

My Goals

1 Talk about my favorite television programs
2 Ask about others' favorite television programs
3 Express the sequence of occurrence between two actions or events
4 Recognize some homophones (characters sharing the same pronunciation but have different meanings)
5 Become familiar with vocabulary associated with televiaion programs

diàn shì jī
电视(机)

jié mù biǎo
节目表

xīn wén
新闻

kǎ tōng
卡通

diàn yǐng
电影

lián xù jù
连续剧
(soap opera, drama series)

 Play It

1 In small groups, discuss and come up with a list of shows that fall under the categories of television programs above.

2 Send a representative up front to present the list of shows your group has compiled.

3 The teacher will then write down the categories as headings on the board.

4 As a group, send another representative to stand in front of the board. The teacher will randomly name a television show. The representatives in front decide which category the show belongs to and try to be the first to tap the accurate heading on the board. The fastest group wins.

New Words

| diàn shì jī
电视(机) television | jié mù biǎo
节目表 program schedule | xīn wén
新闻 news | kǎ tōng
卡通 cartoon | diàn yǐng
电影 movie |

dǎ kāi diàn shì jié mù
打开电视节目多，

xīn wén kǎ tōng jiā diàn yǐng
新闻卡通加电影，

yīng wén xuǎn
英文中文自己选，

jiǔ
可是不要看太久。

New Words

dǎ kāi 打开 turn on	jié mù 节目 program	jiā 加 and; add
yīng wén 英文 English	xuǎn 选 choose	jiǔ 久 long

Let's Learn GRAMMAR

很久 (jiǔ)

我找了很久(jiǔ)，还是找不到图书馆。

弟弟选了很久，还是选不到想看的电影。
(xuǎn)(jiǔ)(xuǎn)(diàn yǐng)

小贵学了很久，英文还是说不好。
(jiǔ)(yīng wén)

小明写了很久，作业还是写不完。
(jiǔ)

> **TIP**
> "很……" is an objective expression specifying the degree to which the following adjective applies. "太……" is a subjective expression, suggesting that the degree of the adjective that follows is much greater than desired.

太久 (jiǔ)

电视不要看得太久。
(diàn shì)(jiǔ)

弟弟电视看得太久了，所以作业还没写完。
(diàn shì)(jiǔ)

小明打球打得太久了，所以还没回家吃晚饭。
(jiǔ)

你　看哪个节目，　我　就　看哪个节目。
<small>jié mù</small>　　　　　　　　　　<small>jié mù</small>

他看什么电影，我就看什么电影。
<small>diàn yǐng</small>　　　　　<small>diàn yǐng</small>

同学买哪本书，他就买哪本书。

哥哥喝哪种果汁，妹妹就喝哪种果汁。
<small>zhǒng</small>　　　　　　<small>zhǒng</small>

同学选什么课，我就选什么课。
<small>xuǎn</small>　　　　　<small>xuǎn</small>

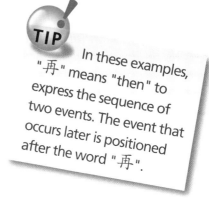

TIP This is a sentence structure where the second clause replicates the first clause. The question tag (什么,哪个……) does not have any interrogative function and varies according to the noun following it.

看完电影，　再　去图书馆。
<small>diàn yǐng</small>

吃完饭，再喝果汁。

写完作业，再看电视。
　　　　　　<small>diàn shì</small>

跳完舞，再吃饭。

TIP In these examples, "再" means "then" to express the sequence of two events. The event that occurs later is positioned after the word "再".

New Words

<small>zhǒng</small>
种 kind, type

Go300

WANT TO LEARN MORE?

Check out the Text > Sentence Pattern section in the Go300 CD.

Find a partner and practice the following dialogues.

⭐Task 1

A: 你想看什么电视节目？
diàn shì jié mù

B: 你看哪个节目，我就看哪个节目。
jié mù　　　　　　　　jié mù

A: 我想看电影。
diàn yǐng

B: 你想看中文电影还是英文电影？
diàn yǐng　　　　　yīng wén diàn yǐng

A: 我想看＿＿＿＿＿＿＿＿＿＿＿＿。

⭐Task 2

A: 我喜欢看卡通，有的卡通很好笑(amusing)。
kǎ tōng　　　　　kǎ tōng　　hǎo xiào

B: 我弟弟也喜欢看卡通。可是妈妈要弟弟做完
kǎ tōng
功课，再看卡通。
kǎ tōng

A: 我妈妈也要我们做完功课，再看电视。上个
diàn shì
星期，我们看电视看得太久了，妈妈很生气。
diàn shì　　　jiǔ

 **Task 3**

A : 我每天都看一个小时的电视新闻，
　　dià n shì xī n wén

你看不看新闻？
xī n wén

B : 我也常常看新闻。
xī n wén

A : 你什么时候看新闻？
xī n wén

B : 我吃完晚饭就会看新闻。
xī n wén

Task 4

A : 你常常看电视吗？
dià n shì

B : ＿＿＿＿＿＿＿＿＿＿＿＿。

A : 你什么时候看电视？
dià n shì

B : ＿＿＿＿＿＿＿＿＿＿＿＿。

A : 你最喜欢看什么电视节目？
dià n shì jié mù

B : ＿＿＿＿＿＿＿＿＿＿＿＿。

The following dialogues are adapted from the Text > Dialogue section in your **Go300**. Listen to the CD before reading the transcript on this page.

⭐ Task 5

Ⓐ : 你喜欢看什么节目？
_{jié mù}

Ⓑ : 我喜欢看卡通，每天下午四点半都有卡通。
_{kǎ tōng}　　　　　　　　　　　　　　　　_{kǎ tōng}

⭐ Task 6

Ⓐ : 你想看哪个节目？请你自己选。
_{jié mù}　　　　　　　　_{xuǎn}

Ⓑ : 没关系，你看哪个节目，我就看哪个节目。
_{jié mù}　　　　　　　　　_{jié mù}

⭐ Task 7

Ⓐ : 你在家看中文电视还是英文电视？
_{diàn shì}　　　_{yīng wén diàn shì}

Ⓑ : 爷爷奶奶他们看中文的，我们看英文的。
_{yīng wén}

⭐ Task 8

Ⓐ : 你看了今天的新闻了吗？
_{xīn wén}

Ⓑ : 还没有，有什么大新闻？
_{xīn wén}

Any hot news?

Let's Learn CHARACTER

Due to the morphology and the way characters were formed in the Chinese language, homophones (characters with the same pronunciation) are very common. There may be fewer homophones in other languages which use the alphabetical system of writing and pronunciation. Hence, a foreign learner of Chinese may be prone to confusion if he cannot tell the difference between homophones. In the following, we look at some homophones we have learnt before. Study them and note the differences—although they are pronounced the same way, there are vast differences in their morphology and their meanings.

TIP

In Chinese, "书" and "输" sound the same. Hence, it is considered bad luck by some Chinese to receive a book as a present because it is thought that the present might bring about a loss to the recipient.

Practice It

Which of the following characters share the same *pinyin*? Write down the *pinyin* and the characters in the spaces below.

pinyin	*pinyin*	*pinyin*
characters	**characters**	**characters**

Read the following text carefully.

弟弟说：电视(diàn shì)是他的学校，他可以天天上学，不休息。因为天天都有不同又好看的电视节目(diàn shì jié mù)。有英文节目(yīng wén jié mù)、中文节目(jié mù)，可以学英文(yīng wén)，也可以学中文。天天在家看电视(diàn shì)，电视不用接送，也不用教他，他可以自己学，又方便又好玩。

你说，弟弟说得对不对？

Answer these questions in Chinese.

1 What does the author's brother say his school is?

2 Why does he say he could go to school every day?

3 What does "可以学英文，也可以学中文" mean?

4 Who does "自己" in the phrase "他可以自己学" refer to?

Read the following text carefully.

dǎ kāi diàn shì xīn wén
爸爸一下班回家，就打开电视看新闻；

dǎ kāi diàn shì
哥哥一下课回家，就打开电视看球赛；

dǎ kāi diàn shì diàn yǐng
姐姐一下课回家，就打开电视看电影；

dǎ kāi diàn shì kǎ tōng
弟弟一下课回家，就打开电视看卡通；

妈妈叫："吃饭了。"没有人回答。

Answer these questions in Chinese.

1   What television programs does the author's family enjoy?
    Write them down in the table below.

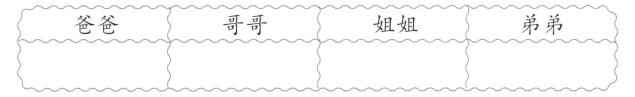

爸爸	哥哥	姐姐	弟弟

2   What does the author's mother want everybody to do?

3   At the end of this passage, nobody responds to the author's mother. What do you think happens next?
    Try writing an ending to this story before checking out the ending in the CD (Text > Reading: 2-1).

WANT TO LEARN MORE?

Check out the Text > Reading section in the Go300 CD.

1 Using the dialogue below, find out which category of television programs your classmates enjoy and how long they spend watching television every day. Record your findings in the table below.

2 Each group has to send a representative to the front to report the group's findings.

Ⓐ： 你最喜欢看什么电视节目？
diàn shì jié mù

Ⓑ： 我最喜欢看电影。
diàn yǐng

Ⓐ： 你每天看多久(how long)电视？
duō jiǔ diàn shì

Ⓑ： 我每天都看两个小时的电视。
diàn shì

Name	Categories of television shows he or she enjoys	Duration spent on watching television every day

3. As an individual assignment, tally the findings of all the groups and find out the category most of your classmates enjoy. Write it down in the blank below.

Category enjoyed by most of my classmates: [　　　　　]

LEARNING LOG

I can...	Excellent	Good	Fair	Needs Improvement
1 name the categories of common television programs.	☐	☐	☐	☐
2 name and talk about my favorite television programs, and ask about others' favorite television programs.	☐	☐	☐	☐
3 use the sentence structures "……，就……", and "……，再……" appropriately.	☐	☐	☐	☐
4 identify homophones such as "是", "事", "市", "视", and "书", "输".	☐	☐	☐	☐
5 write "视", "目", "新", "英", and "通".	☐	☐	☐	☐

今天天气
The Weather Today

San Francisco
54-57°F/
12-14°C

Paris
59-79°F/
15-26°C

Beijing
66-86°F/
19-30°C

Cairo
75-100°F/
24-38°C

Rio De Janeiro
55-72°F/
13-22°C

Sydney
48-64°F/
9-18°C

My Goals

1 Describe the weather

2 Describe feelings of hot and cold

3 Illustrate in my sentences that an action is ongoing, or that two actions are occurring concurrently

4 Use the semicolon " ： " appropriately

5 Become familiar with vocabulary associated with the weather

Get Started

tài yáng
太阳

guā fēng
刮风

Play It

Charades: Send representatives from each group one by one to the teacher for a word or phrase. The representative has to act out the word or phrase and the rest of the class will try to figure it out. The group that guesses it first wins.

yáng guāng
阳光

xià yǔ
下雨

wū yún
乌云
(dark clouds)

rè
热

qíng tiān
晴天

yǔ tiān
雨天
(rainy day)

yīn tiān
阴天

lěng
冷

New Words

tài yáng 太阳 sun	yáng guāng 阳光 sunshine	qíng tiān 晴天 sunny day	guā fēng 刮风 wind blowing
xià yǔ 下雨 rain	yīn tiān 阴天 cloudy day; overcast day	rè 热 hot	lěng 冷 cold

Let's CHANT Go300

花，喜欢阳光，看着阳光笑；
yáng guāng　　zhe yáng guāng xiào

草，喜欢下雨，张着嘴喝水；
xià yǔ　　zhāng zhe

树，喜欢刮风，唱着歌跳舞。
shù　　guā fēng　　zhe

Think About It

Some people are cheered up by sunny days while rainy days depress them. Yet others are heartened by rainy days. What kind of weather do you like? Are your moods influenced by weather changes?

New Words

着 (an adverbial particle)	笑 laugh	张着 open	树 tree
zhe	xiào	zhāng zhe	shù

Let's Learn GRAMMAR

着 *(zhe)*

哥哥唱着歌，妹妹跳着舞， *(zhe)* *(zhe)*

大家玩得很开心。

弟弟张着嘴想唱歌，可是他不会唱。 *(zhāng zhe)*

> "着" in this instance indicates that an action is still on-going.

> **TIP** There are two meanings to "着". Where it means the simultaneity of two actions, it has the same meaning as suggested in the sentence structure "一边……，一边……".
> For example, "姑姑听着音乐跳舞。" means the same as "姑姑一边听音乐，一边跳舞。".

姑姑听着音乐跳舞。 *(zhe)*

> "着" in this instance indicates that two actions are happening simultaneously: listening to music and dancing at the same time.

老师看着我说："明天不要忘了交作业。" *(zhe)*

爸爸喜欢晴天，他看着阳光笑。 *(qíng tiān)* *(zhe yáng guāng xiào)*

……怎么样？

今天天气怎么样？

他的心情怎么样？

你昨天看的电影怎么样？

这个星期日去看球赛怎么样？

> **TIP** Here, "怎么样?" is used to ask somebody about a situation or for his opinion.

会

A: 明天会很<ruby>热<rt>rè</rt></ruby>吗？

B: 我想明天会很<ruby>热<rt>rè</rt></ruby>。

A: 明天你会很忙吗？

B: 明天我又要打球，又要参加乐队，

我会很忙。

TIP "会 + Adjective" indicates the possibility of a condition or situation.

"会 + Verb" indicates the capability of a person, often through some training or practice.

For example:
➤ 妹妹会唱歌。
➤ 弟弟会跳舞。

明天天气好，	我们	就	去打球。

<ruby>刮风或<rt>guā fēng huò</rt></ruby> (or) <ruby>下雨<rt>xià yǔ</rt></ruby>，我就不去看电影。

没事做，我就会去打球。

有<ruby>地图<rt>dì tú</rt></ruby> (map)，我就找得到图书馆。

TIP These are hypothetical sentences which contain two clauses each. The clause which is led by "就" introduces the outcome that will follow only after the conditions in the preceding clause are met. The hypothetical tag "如果" or "要是 (if)" is omitted at the beginning of the sentences.

Go300

WANT TO LEARN MORE?

Check out the Text > Sentence Pattern section in the Go300 CD.

Find a partner and practice the following dialogues.

★ Task 1

Ⓐ: 我每天都看电视新闻。

Ⓑ: 你为什么每天看新闻？

Ⓐ: 看新闻可以知道_{zhī dào}(know)很多不同的事，
还可以知道_{zhī dào}明天的天气。

Ⓑ: 明天有棒球比赛，会下雨_{xià yǔ}吗？

Ⓐ: 你看新闻就知道_{zhī dào}了。

★ Task 2

Ⓐ: 今天外面_{wài miàn}冷_{lěng}不冷_{lěng}？

Ⓑ: 今天天气很好，外面_{wài miàn}不冷_{lěng}也不热_{rè}。

Ⓐ: 下午你有事吗？你想不想去打球？

Ⓑ: 下午我没事。你想打什么球？

Ⓐ: 我们去打棒球怎么样？

Ⓑ: 好，我喜欢打棒球。

New Words

外面 wài miàn outside

⭐ Task 3

Ⓐ 你喜欢晴天还是雨天？
qíng tiān · yǔ tiān

Ⓑ 我喜欢晴天，晴天我可以
qíng tiān · qíng tiān

在草地上看书。你也喜欢

晴天吗？
qíng tiān

Ⓐ 晴天、雨天我都喜欢。
qíng tiān · yǔ tiān

我们一起去散步，好不好？

Ⓑ 现在外面下着雨，我不想去。等一等，
wài miàn xià zhe yǔ

不下雨了，我就和你一起去散步。
xià yǔ

⭐ Task 4

Ⓐ 春天、夏天、秋天和冬天，我最喜欢夏天。

Ⓑ 我不喜欢夏天，因为夏天太热了。
rè

Ⓒ 我最喜欢冬天。冬天天气冷，会下雪。
lěng

我喜欢玩雪球(snow ball)。
xuě qiú

Ⓓ 我最喜欢＿＿＿＿＿＿＿＿＿＿。

Task 5

Complete the dialogues below according to the pictures. When you have done that, listen to the Text > Dialogue Section in your  Go300 to compare your answers.

Ⓐ 明天天气怎么样？

Ⓑ : _____

Ⓐ 你明天会不会来
打球？

Ⓑ : _____

③

Ⓐ 明天lěng · lěng冷不冷？

Ⓑ : _____

④

Ⓐ 明天会很rè热吗？

Ⓑ : _____

LESSON 10

Let's Learn PUNCTUATION

fēn hào

；分号
(semicolon)

The semicolon is often used between two semantically-connected sentences that either parallel or contrast each other. The semicolon is also commonly used at the end of a multi-clausal sentence to sum up the content of the entire sentence.

yáng guāng　zhe yáng guāng xiào　xià yǔ
花，喜欢阳光，看著阳光笑；草，喜欢下雨，
zhāng zhe
张著嘴喝水。

tài yáng　xià yǔ
明天出太阳，我们就去球场打球；下雨，我们
就在家里玩游戏。

xià yǔ　shù　yǔ　shù　guā fēng
下雨，树很开心，雨和树一起玩游戏；刮风，
shù　fēng　shù
树很开心，风和树一起跳舞。

我有眼睛可以看，我有耳朵可以听，我有手
可以做事；这就是幸福。

Practice It

Fill in the blanks with the correct punctuation marks.

1. 张开眼睛□可以看□张开嘴□可以问问题□
2. 你姓张□他姓张□我也姓张□我们的姓都一样□
3. yáng guāng　qíng tiān　wū yún　yīn tiān　xià yǔ
有阳光□是晴天□有乌云□是阴天□下雨了□
yǔ tiān
是雨天□

Read the following text carefully.

爸爸开车送我去学校，他开着车，我唱着歌，zhe zhe
他笑着问我：xiào zhe"喜欢上学吗？"

我笑着回答：xiào zhe"喜欢上学，我喜欢我的老师，
喜欢我的同学，也喜欢学校的活动。"

我笑着问爸爸：xiào zhe"喜欢上班吗？"

爸爸也笑着回答：xiào zhe"喜欢上班，上班有事做，
上班有钱赚。"

爸爸笑着说，我笑着听，xiào zhe xiào zhe我们一起唱歌，真是
开心的一天。

Answer these questions in Chinese.

1 Where does the above conversation take place? Besides talking, what else are the author and his father doing?

2 Do you think the author and his father are in a good mood? Why?

3 Does the author like to go to school? Why?

WANT TO LEARN MORE?

Check out the Text > Reading section in the Go300 CD.

Text 2

Read the following text carefully.

风*和太阳常常吵架。

风一边吹*着，一边说：“我是最强*的。”太阳听了很不开心，太阳想：“我才*是最强的。”风对太阳说：“我们来比赛，怎么样？”太阳说：“太好了！你看，地上有一个穿着大衣*的人，我们来比一比，看谁能脱掉*他的大衣。”

风用力*吹着，吹了很久很久，还是没有用。太阳出来了，地上的人看着太阳说：“今天的太阳真大，天气真热。”说完，就脱掉大衣了。

* 风 wind   * 吹 blow   * 强 strong   * 才 only (used for intensifying the tone)

* 大衣 coat   * 脱掉 take off   * 用力 to exert (strength, force)

Answer these questions in Chinese.

1 What are the wind and the sun arguing about?

2 What do the wind and the sun do respectively to get the passerby to take off his coat?

3 Who is the winner in the end?

Weather Report

NEW YORK

5月20日	5月21日	5月22日	5月23日	5月24日	5月25日	5月26日
50-80°F	53-73°F	53-69°F	55-71°F	55-71°F	55-71°F	55-73°F

1 Students will be divided into small groups. Each group will be in charge of finding out the weather forecast of a designated city for the coming week (as illustrated in the diagram above).

2 Create computer presentation slides or posters based on your findings. In a group, present the weather forecast to your class in the manner of a newscaster. Your report should include the following information:

(1) Name of city

(2) Dates of the forecast

(3) Number of clear and cloudy days in the week; number of days of rain or snow in the week

(4) The hottest and coldest days in the week

3 Students will vote for the group with the most comprehensive report, as well as the group which displays the most creativity in its preparation and presentation.

LEARNING LOG

I can...

	Excellent	Good	Fair	Needs Improvement
1 talk about daily weather conditions in Chinese.	☐	☐	☐	☐
2 describe feelings of hot and cold according to how I feel.	☐	☐	☐	☐
3 use "着" to illustrate that an action is ongoing, or to describe two actions that are occurring concurrently.	☐	☐	☐	☐
4 use the semicolon " ; " between two parallel or contrasting sentences.	☐	☐	☐	☐
5 write "阳", "着", "笑", "风", and "雨".	☐	☐	☐	☐

Vocabulary Index

Words indicated with an asterisk (*) are supplementary vocabulary from each lesson. They are included to supplement students' vocabulary and enhance their oral proficiency.

Pinyin	Simplified Character	English	Traditional Character	Lesson
A				
ài hào	爱好	hobby	愛好	L8
B				
bàng qiú	棒球	baseball		L7
bào gào	报告*	report	報告	L3
bí shuǐ	鼻水	mucus		L4
bǐ	比	compare		L7
bǐ sài	比赛	contest	比賽	L7
biǎo dì	表弟	younger cousin (male, both paternal and maternal)		L1
biǎo gē	表哥	older cousin (male, both paternal and maternal)		L1
biǎo jiě	表姐	older cousin (female, both paternal and maternal)	表姊	L1
biǎo mèi	表妹	younger cousin (female, both paternal and maternal)		L1
bìng rén	病人*	patient		L4
bó bo	伯伯	uncle (father's older brother)		L1
bó mǔ	伯母*	aunt (wife of father's older brother)		L1
C				
cān jiā	参加	join; participate in	參加	L2
cháng cháng	常常	often		L8
chǎng	场	(a measure word used for a contest)	場	L7
chàng gē	唱歌	sing a song		L8
chǎo jià	吵架	quarrel		L6
chéng jì	成绩	grades	成績	L3
chéng jì dān	成绩单*	school report card	成績單	L3
chī yào	吃药*	take medicine	吃藥	L4
chū lái	出来	come out	出來	L4
chū qù	出去	go out		L4
cì	次	time; instance		L8

D

dǎ jià	打架	fight		L6
dǎ kāi	打开	turn on	打開	L9
dà kǎo	大考	final examination		L3
dài	带	bring	带	L6
de	得	(a particle used after a verb or an adjective to express possibility or capability)		L3
děi	得	have to		L2
diàn shì (jī)	电视(机)	television	電視(機)	L9
diàn yǐng	电影	movie	電影	L9
dù zi tòng	肚子痛*	stomachache		L4
...duì	……队	team ...	……隊	L7
duì miàn	对面	opposite	對面	L5

E

ér zi	儿子	son	兒子	L1

F

fā shāo	发烧*	fever	發燒	L4
fàn guǎn	饭馆	restaurant	飯館	L5
fāng biàn	方便	convenient		L5
fēn	分	score		L7
fù jìn	附近	nearby		L5

G

gěi	给	give	給	L2
gōng yuán	公园*	park	公園	L5
gū gu	姑姑	aunt (father's sister)		L1
gū fù	姑父*	uncle (husband of father's sister)		L1
guā fēng	刮风	wind blowing	颳風	L10

H

hài pà	害怕*	scared		L6
hē shuǐ	喝水*	drink water		L4
hé chàng tuán	合唱团*	choir	合唱團	L2
hù shi	护士*	nurse	護士	L4
huà huà	画画*	paint	畫畫	L8

huài	坏	bad	壞	L3
huí jiā	回家	go home		L2

J

jiā	加	and; add		L9
jiāo	交	hand in		L3
jié mù	节目	program	節目	L9
jié mù biǎo	节目表	program schedule	節目表	L9
jìn	近	close, near		L5
jǐn zhāng	紧张	nervous	緊張	L7
jīng cǎi	精彩	outstanding, fantastic		L7
jiǔ	久	long		L9
jiù jiu	舅舅	uncle (mother's brother)		L1
jiù mā	舅妈*	aunt (wife of mother's brother)	舅媽	L1

K

kǎ tōng	卡通	cartoon		L9
kāi xīn	开心	happy	開心	L6
kàn bìng	看病	see a doctor		L5
kàn diàn yǐng	看电影*	watch a movie	看電影	L8
kǎo	考	take an exam		L3
kǎo juàn	考卷*	test paper		L3
kǎo shì	考试*	examination	考試	L3
ké	咳	cough		L4
ké sou	咳嗽	cough		L4
kě shì	可是	but, however		L2
kè wài huó dòng	课外活动	extra-curricular activity	課外活動	L2
kū	哭*	cry		L6

L

lā lā duì	拉拉队*	cheerleading	啦啦隊	L2
lán qiú	篮球	basketball	籃球	L7
lěng	冷	cold		L10
lí	离	be away from	離	L5
lián xù jù	连续剧*	soap opera, drama series	連續劇	L9
liáo tiān	聊天*	chat		L8
liú	流	flow	流	L4

liú bí shuǐ	流鼻水	running nose	流鼻水	L4
liú bí tì	流鼻涕	running nose	流鼻涕	L4
M				
mà rén	骂人	scold	罵人	L6
mǎi cài	买菜	buy vegetables or groceries	買菜	L5
měi cì	每次	every time		L8
měi lì	美丽	beautiful	美麗	L6
měi shì zú qiú	美式足球*	American Football		L7
N				
nǎi nai	奶奶	grandmother (paternal)		L1
nán	男	male		L1
nán guò	难过	miserable/sad	難過	L4/L6
nán kàn	难看	terrible, ugly	難看	L6
nǚ ér	女儿	daughter	女兒	L1
P				
pǎo bù	跑步	run, jog		L8
péng you	朋友	friend		L8
piào	票	ticket		L7
pīng pāng qiú	乒乓球	table tennis		L7
Q				
qí yì shè	棋艺社*	chess club	棋藝社	L2
qíng tiān	晴天	sunny day		L10
qiú chǎng	球场	court for ball games (basketball, tennis, etc.)	球場	L5
qiú duì	球队	ball team	球隊	L2
qiú sài	球赛	ball game	球賽	L7
R				
rè	热	hot	熱	L10
S				
shāng diàn	商店*	store		L5
shàng kè	上课	go to class	上課	L2
shěn shen	婶婶*	aunt (wife of father's younger brother)	嬸嬸	L1
shēng bìng	生病	sick		L4
shēng qì	生气	angry	生氣	L6
shí hou	时候	time	時候	L3

shì chǎng	市场	market	市場	L5
shū	输	lose	輸	L7
shū fǎ	书法	calligraphy	書法	L8
shū shu	叔叔	uncle (father's younger brother)		L1
shù	树	tree	樹	L10
shuǐ	水	water		L4
sòng	送	give (as a present)		L2
sūn nǚ	孙女	granddaughter (son's daughter)	孫女	L1
sūn zi	孙子	grandson (son's son)	孫子	L1
suǒ yǐ	所以	so	所以	L6
T				
tài yáng	太阳	sun	太陽	L10
táng gē	堂哥	older cousin (male, paternal)		L1
táng mèi	堂妹	younger cousin (female, paternal)		L1
tiào wǔ	跳舞	dance		L8
tīng yīn yuè	听音乐*	listen to music	聽音樂	L8
tíng chē	停车	park (a vehicle)	停車	L5
tíng chē chǎng	停车场	parking lot	停車場	L5
tóng	同	the same		L1
tú shū guǎn	图书馆	library	圖書館	L5
W				
wài gōng	外公	grandfather (maternal)		L1
wài miàn	外面	outside		L10
wài pó	外婆	grandmother (maternal)		L1
wài sūn	外孙	grandson (daughter's son)	外孫	L1
wài sūn nǚ	外孙女	granddaughter (daugter's daughter)	外孫女	L1
wán	完	finished		L3
wǎng qiú	网球*	tennis	網球	L7
wèi shén me	为什么	why, what for	為什麼	L6
wū yún	乌云*	dark clouds	烏雲	L10
X				
xǐ huan	喜欢	like	喜歡	L7
xià kè	下课	end of class	下課	L2
xià yǔ	下雨	rain		L10

xiǎng	想	want		L2
xiàng	向	to		L5
xiàng qián	向前	forward		L5
xiàng qián zǒu	向前走*	go ahead		L5
xiàng yòu zhuǎn	向右转*	turn right	向右轉	L5
xiàng zuǒ zhuǎn	向左转*	turn left	向左轉	L5
xiǎo kǎo	小考	quiz		L3
xiǎo shí	小时	hour	小時	L8
xiào	笑	laugh		L6*/L10
xiě zuò yè	写作业*	do homework	寫作業	L3
xīn qíng	心情	mood		L6
xīn wén	新闻	news	新聞	L9
xiū xi	休息	rest		L2
xuǎn	选	choose	選	L9
xué shēng huì	学生会*	student union	學生會	L2
xué xiào	学校	school	學校	L2
Y				
yá tòng	牙痛*	toothache		L4
yáng guāng	阳光	sunshine	陽光	L10
yào	药	medicine	藥	L4
yé ye	爷爷	grandfather (paternal)	爺爺	L1
yī shēng	医生	doctor	醫生	L4
yī yuàn	医院	hospital	醫院	L5
yí mā	姨妈	aunt (mother's sister)	姨媽	L1
yí fù	姨父*	uncle (husband of mother's sister)		L1
yì jiā rén	一家人	the whole family		L1
yì biān... yì biān...	一边……, 一边……	do the things at the same time	一邊……, 一邊……	L8
yīn tiān	阴天	cloudy day; overcast day	陰天	L10
yīn wèi	因为	because	因為	L6
yīn yuè	音乐	music	音樂	L8
yīng wén	英文	English	英文	L9
yíng	赢	win	赢	L7
yòng xīn	用心	pay attention		L3
yóu jú	邮局*	post office	郵局	L5

yòu zhuǎn	右转	turn right	右轉	L5
yǔ tiān	雨天*	rainy day		L10
yuè duì	乐队	music band	樂隊	L2
yùn dòng	运动	exercise	運動	L7
Z				
zěn me	怎么	how	怎麼	L4
zhāng zhe	张着	open	張著	L10
zhe	着	(an adverbial particle)	著	L10
zhǒng	种	kind, type	種	L9
zhòng yào	重要	important		L3
zhù	住	live		L5
zhuō qiú	桌球	billiards; table tennis (in certain Chinese regions)		L7
zì jǐ	自己	self		L6
zú qiú	足球*	soccer		L7
zuì	最	most		L3
zuǒ zhuǎn	左转	turn left	左轉	L5
zuò yè	作业	homework	作業	L3